Developing Great Managers
20 "POWER HOUR"
Conversations
That Build Skills Fast

Lisa Haneberg

PRESS
Alexandria, Virginia

ASTD Press is an internationally renowned source of insightful and practical information on workplace learning and performance topics, including training basics, evaluation and return on investment, instructional systems development, e-learning, leadership, and career development.

Ordering information: Books published by ASTD Press can be purchased by visiting our Website at store.astd.org or by calling 800.628.2783 or 703.683.8100.

Library of Congress Control Number: 2007931352

ISBN-10: 1-56286-501-3
ISBN-13: 978-1-56286-501-6

ASTD Press Editorial Staff:
Director: Cat Russo
Manager, Acquisitions and Author Relations: Mark Morrow
Editorial Manager: Jacqueline Edlund-Braun
Editorial Assistant: Maureen Soyars
Retail Trade Manager: Yelba Quinn
Content Development, Design, and Composition by Aptara, Falls Church,
    Virginia, www.aptaracorp.com
    Developmental Editor: Robin C. Bonner
    Interior Designer: Carol Bleistine
    Indexer: Dorothy M. Jahoda
Cover Design: Renita Wade
Cover Photograph: © zeit für frühstük. Roy Hans-Joachim

Printed by Victor Graphics, Inc., Baltimore, Maryland,
www.victorgraphics.com

CONTENTS

Contents

PREFACE

I believe that management is a craft—developed and built over time and with great care. Great managers link goals with results and facilitate the flow of work. They are the get-it-done people, and they can make a significant positive impact on business results. Being a manager is challenging. Managers deal with ever-changing demands, ambiguous priorities, barriers, breakdowns, and a full range of human emotions. Great managers are gifted in many ways and disciplines.

If your business results are unsatisfactory, I would assess the strategies and then see if your implementation engine—management—needs tuning. I like thinking about managers as the *implementation engine* because the term helps punctuate their importance. Often, however, the management function is not aligned to produce optimal results. You will want to ensure that management jobs are defined and clarified, and then you will want to make sure you arm your managers with the best tools and techniques possible.

I have never been a fan of academy-type training for managers. Going to one week of training per year is nice, but it might not serve your participants or the company as well as a more applied and integrated approach. Like other crafts, management needs constant care and feeding, not inoculations. This book is designed to help you create a learning environment that will help your managers excel. As you use this book, please remember that you cannot do any class once—no matter how great it is—and declare your managers trained and ready. It would be nice if it were that simple. More care and attention is required to stoke the fires of the management engine. That said, I find that some of the very best management training solutions are also easy to share and implement.

I have been a management and leadership trainer for over 25 years and have seen management training done many ways—from a formal university concept to a learn-on-your-own approach of abdication. This book offers ideas for ways to create effective and sustainable results with an approach that is neither of these things but uses the best elements of both. I hope you enjoy putting Power Hours to work for you.

Lisa Haneberg
Seattle, Washington
February 2008

Developing Great Managers

CHAPTER 1

How to Get the Most Out of This Book

What's Covered in This Chapter

- ❖ Why management training requires an applied approach
- ❖ Target audience for this book
- ❖ What's included in this workbook

Organizations struggle to ensure that their managers learn and grow. The managers needing the most help are often those least likely to receive training—because they are so busy, they can't attend traditional, day-long classes. In addition, workplace demands change more rapidly than the training curriculum can. Training departments are challenged to present relevant material while also keeping costs down—two goals that are often in conflict with one another. Virtual training can be useful, but developing professional online learning is costly and it takes time.

Trainers are faced with the most troubling challenge of all—the ability to connect with and engage their audience during training sessions. If managers are to take charge of their own development and improvement, they need to be engaged. Unless the training facilitator is extraordinary, canned programs bought from the best names in the business for thousands of dollars will not provide the one simple thing that managers need most: A great conversation about the business and how they can better manage their people.

Learning needs to be about *the conversation*. For trainers, this idea offers a great opportunity, as well as several challenges. Trainers have the opportunity to become powerful catalysts for enlivening great business conversations. After training others for more than 25 years, I now realize that this is the most valuable thing I can do for an organization and its managers. The challenge comes when we try to determine how to enliven business conversations about management. The not-so-simple (albeit liberating) answer is, "everywhere and in all ways!" Management training is moving into a new realm that feels a little nostalgic. We are getting back to basics: We focus on creating connecting conversations whereby managers learn about techniques and practices that can help them do their jobs. We have a few new tools to create these conversations, such as podcasts and blogs, but otherwise we feel like we are getting back to the old days of a more "salon approach" to learning (deep, provocative, informal conversations where the leader changes with the topic).

This focus on connection and conversation is mirrored in other aspects of business, as well, such as the use of weblogs and websites that allow customers to interact with each other and company personnel. The workplace is becoming more transparent and authentic, and our training programs should reinforce these same themes and values.

Many training resources offer managers full-day or week-long training agendas. In this workbook, I decided to offer 20 one-hour conversations to help you play more fully in the informal training space. You will find that the rewards for completing shorter and more evocative training sessions are greater than those gained while attending lengthier, more traditional training classes. Your managers will love you, too, because they will find that these short sessions are easier to fit into their busy days, and they will work—Power Hours help managers manage better.

Target Audience

I wrote this book for management trainers. Middle and senior managers will also find it useful for management team development. I'm aware that not every company has the luxury of professional management trainers on staff. This workbook will help *anyone* in the position of helping managers grow and develop.

If you work for a *Fortune* 500 company and are looking for resources to build a corporate university program for managers, this workbook will not tell you how to do it. I do recommend, however, that even if your organization offers a separate and more formal training program, you give these Power Hours a try. They will keep managers connected between larger training events and reinforce your key messages.

Scope of This Book

The first four chapters of *Developing Great Managers: 20 "Power Hours" That Build Skills Fast* contain general information about management training and lead up to the 20 Management Training Power Hours found in chapters 7 through 26. Please don't skip these beginning chapters because in them I offer suggestions for ways to prepare your managers and to make the sessions a success. In addition, if you want to understand the philosophical foundations for the program design and my beliefs about management training, read chapter 3. I would particularly recommend familiarizing yourself with the section on Management Training Theory (chapter 2) and skills every management trainer should have (chapter 3).

The facilitator's guidelines for the 20 Management Training Power Hours can be found in part 3 the Power Hour chapters, 7 through 26. Although the trainee handouts are included in those chapters, they are listed in the Appendix and appear again in 8½ × 11 format on the CD packaged with the book, so they are easy for you to modify and print. The materials are simple and low-tech by design—I want the focus to be on *the conversation,* not the flashy presentation or other bells and whistles!

What to Do Next

❖ Spend some time reflecting on the goals you have for your management training.

❖ Use your goals as a filter as you read about and consider using the Management Training Power Hours.

CHAPTER 2

How to Help Managers Learn and Grow

What's Covered in This Chapter

- ❖ Assumptions we have about how adults learn
- ❖ Beliefs we have about how managers learn
- ❖ Downsides of control
- ❖ Understanding the 10 factors that enhance learning and how to apply that knowledge

Theories of Adult Learning and Management Training

Managers are adults, so it makes sense to apply the basic assumptions of adult learning to the art and practice of training managers. As a reminder, see the sidebar on basic assumptions and

Adult Learning Basics

✓ Adult learners need to feel that the new information and skills directly link to and benefit their goals. Their hearts and minds *both* need to be engaged in the learning process.

✓ Adult learners respond well to real-world examples and applications. Be sure to talk with trainees about how the principles and practices relate to their own management situations!

✓ Adult learners resist forced attendance at training sessions. They want to come up with ideas for learning and development on their own or be able to choose from a list of options. Trainers should refrain from prescribing training or development. Instead, they should have open conversations with trainees and ask questions that allow the trainees to discover and determine their development options.

✓ Adult learners may be on the defensive or feel attacked when their supervisor recommends training. Put your trainees in control: Ask them to define their goals, as well as the information or skills that would most help them reach their goals.

✓ Adult learners are invested in their careers and successes. They may be reluctant to share their mistakes or weaknesses. Help trainees find the learning environments that work for them and redefine success so that open discussions and learning evoke less fear and insecurity.

✓ Adult learners own their progresses and welcome clear feedback. Help trainees determine how well their management skills are developing and encourage them to begin to apply new skills immediately.

✓ Adult learners come to training or development sessions with years of previous experiences, opinions, and mind-sets. Ensure that they have the opportunity to share, acknowledge, and move beyond their biases. They will slowly apply concepts and practices that run counter to their usual ways of thinking. Trainers should understand and allow time for this transition.

✓ Adult learners cannot be forced to learn. They must want to be coached, and this is their choice. Help facilitate their progress through open and candid conversations focused on the goals they feel passionately about achieving.

beliefs on how adults learn and how trainers should use this information.

Adults learn differently than children, and trainers need to understand adult learning theory to help trainees build skills and realize their potential growth. These assumptions and beliefs also pertain to management training, but there's more: As a management trainer, you need to be well versed in management training theory (MTT). Here are the main tenants of MTT:

❖ Managers are much too busy! Training must dramatically improve their abilities to succeed or it won't be worth the diversion. In addition, shorter training sessions are easier to fit into a manager's busy day.

❖ Managers often suffer from fuzzy priorities, competing priorities, scope creep, and meeting overload. Management training should acknowledge and assist with these challenges.

❖ Many managers feel overwhelmed and stressed. This can get in the way of the perfectly logical assertions presented at training. The best training programs will reduce feelings of stress and being overwhelmed.

❖ Many managers work well below their capabilities. Often, this is not a problem of not knowing what to do but of not knowing how to manage time. Training the same facts and techniques over and over will not produce change if the problem is not one of understanding the techniques. For managers to try new approaches, they need more training about how to conduct their days and why the techniques are recommended.

How might the success of our management training differ if we believed—and acted in concert with this belief—that a manager's time is precious? I think the difference would be like night and day for some training departments. Trainers need to remember management training theory when setting up classes, sending out email announcements, and scheduling meetings.

Letting Go of Control

Training needs to be as natural and uncontrolled as possible. That's right, uncontrolled—the less we try to control the training, the better it will be. This might be an uncomfortable notion, because as training professionals we are often told we need to control our functions. We need to control our budgets and manage resources, but this control should not eek into our training. *Not* trying to control training is a wonderful thing. It takes some courage and confidence, but it leads to a better outcome. Likewise, not trying to control meetings and projects also leads to a better outcome.

The most effective learning sessions are not polished, practiced, or choreographed ahead of time. The best training sets the stage for something to happen—then lets things happen. Power Hour Manager Training reflects this approach and does not offer scripts or minute-by-minute facilitation instructions. Overly polished material does not enhance the ability of the learner to apply techniques.

You might call this the "salon approach" to training, and I think this is the right method for management development programs. Salons are organic, stimulating, and transformative because they can jump-start conversations that will have sufficient energy behind them to later lead to action. Comments that flow at such "salon-style" training become catalysts for changing how people approach their work. This book offers many ways to create a space for great learning conversations managers.

Ten Factors That Enhance Learning and the Ability to Apply Concepts

We know how adults learn and how managers learn, and we don't want to over control. So, what approach to management training should we use? There are many great ways to enliven managers' minds so that they learn and then practice the techniques they've learned. Great management training offers a combination of qualities and contexts to appeal to diverse learners. These qualities catalyze development. The sidebar shows 10 factors that can improve

Factors That Improve a Manager's Ability to Apply and Habituate Learning

1. Sound Science
2. Star Power
3. Magnetic Trainer
4. Provocation
5. Evocation
6. Connecting Conversation
7. Diversity of Thought
8. Deep Versus Wide
9. Doing a Job
10. Tactile Trying

a manager's ability to apply and habituate learning, which are discussed more fully below.

Sound Science

Training needs to be built on a solid foundation. The techniques need to work. The theories ought to make sense. This may seem intuitive, but some training programs go way off the "weird" scale. Managers don't have time for "mumbo jumbo"—they need real-life concepts and practices that will help them do their jobs *today*. Challenging the status quo is wonderful, but introducing something for the sake of being fun or intellectually stimulating is a waste of time and resources.

Star Power

Let's face it celebrities in the training field sell their concepts well. If your managers can see Marcus Buckingham, Tom Peters, or Benjamin Zander in person (or even on DVD), that has power.

What does this mean? Don't be hesitant to get a famous face to say what you want to say. Open your training with an inspiring DVD, or ask participants to read an article from the *Harvard Business Review* beforehand. There are a lot of famous people saying the same things we are—use that! One caution, though: Resist latching onto gimmicks, acronyms, or "flavor of the month"–type stuff. Managers have become very sick of this stuff and rightly so.

Magnetic Trainer

Are you a magnetic trainer? Magnetic trainers are people with whom others like to hang around at work. They're magnetic because people enjoy talking with them for some reason. Maybe they're fun, interesting, a great listener, empathetic, or super smart. We all have qualities that draw people toward us, and we need to use these attributes to enhance learning. *If people like being with you, they will come to more training sessions and they will participate more fully.* Both introverts and extroverts can be magnetic trainers. Being an awesome listener is a trait that most magnetic trainers are likely to share.

Provocation

Learning often occurs as a result of dissonance—some difference between what we thought was true and another perspective. When our training is provocative, it challenges participants to think in new ways. We should not try to be provocative just to be provocative, however. We need to notice where participants are getting stuck, then offer development that nudges them forward. Something is provocative when it causes a strong reaction. For example, all these emotions might be caused by provocation: annoyance, anger, excitement, fascination, curiosity, or a feeling of invitation. We don't want to routinely anger our training participants, but an occasional bit of anger or frustration, followed by good deep conversation, can be a great learning enhancer.

Evocation

When we are evocative, we help others see things from their own perspective—we put people in the scene for themselves. Evocative learning is very connecting. When people think about a concept or apply it to their situation, they are being evoked. Great training provokes evocation. We want managers to imagine how they will apply the concepts or techniques in their own departments.

Connecting Conversation

Connecting conversation is dialogue that brings concepts, people, and things together. Trainers need to help make connections between what's being discussed in a training class and real business opportunities and challenges. Have you noticed how lively and engaging conversations are when lots of people jump into them and share their unique perspectives? Connecting conversation draws in participation because it is interesting, helpful, and mentally stimulating.

Diversity of Thought

Fill training groups with people who seem to have nothing in common. Oh, what fun it is to bring these diverse perspectives together on one topic! Everyone learns more, and the conversation tends to be both evocative and provocative. Add diverse expert opinions to the mix by having participants read articles with opposing viewpoints before the training session. Diversity is not just interesting and healthy, it's necessary for managers to make good decisions. The training environment is a perfect place to help build an appreciation for diverse thoughts, opinions, and approaches.

Deep Versus Wide

As you will notice throughout this training guide, it is best to address fewer training topics and spend more time on each one.

The deeper you can get into a topic, the deeper will be your learning. Trainers often make the mistake of acquiescing to managers who say they don't have time for training. We pack 12 topics into a one-day training session, knowing all the while that this is not going to lead to a good result. Great training goes deep—it takes time with the concepts and techniques so that managers can make the connection to their work and realize the relevance of the training.

Doing a Job

Great training meets a need. It gets something done. It does a job. When managers need help, there's a job to be done. Training might help fill that need (although it is not always the answer). Our training needs to serve managers, employees, and the organization. If we cannot identify the job we want our training to do, we ought to question whether it's the right training at the right time.

Tactile Trying

Great training invites people to touch it, feel it, and give it a try. Training ought to be a laboratory for safely testing thoughts and techniques. You will notice that most of the exercises in this trainer's manual are based on real-life job tasks and challenges. The best training engages people in working with the material. We should encourage people to take the training apart, then put it back together in the way that best works for them—like a car buff would do to better understand how an engine works.

Wrap-Up

These are 10 factors that enhance learning and one's ability to apply a concept. Think about the next training session you plan to facilitate and how you might be able to strengthen some of these factors for that session. The training recommendations found in this manual also strive to include and blend these enablers to learning. Just like with management training, though, the difference comes not from an intellectual understanding of what to do but from an active attempt to determine how these techniques can enhance all your training efforts—to be able to apply what you've learned. The changes required to help a session go from flat to engaging, from boring to provocative, or from abstract to concrete, are often very small.

What to Do Next

❖ Assess your current and potential training offerings to determine how well they incorporate the "10 Factors That Enhance Management Training."

❖ Reflect on your magnetism as a trainer. How can you be the most fully expressed version of your unique self? Do people seek to be in your company? Why or why not?

❖ Take on the belief that time is precious. In everything you do, question whether it is worth the time it will take managers to participate or respond. Cut down on the number of group emails you send and ensure that every message or handout you distribute serves many purposes.

CHAPTER 3

Create a Culture of Learning

What's Covered in This Chapter

- ❖ Developing a culture of learning
- ❖ Using small amounts of time to make a big impact
- ❖ Identifying skills every management trainer should develop

Creating a Culture of Learning

If you could be a management trainer at a company that had a healthy culture of learning, that would be wonderful, right? As trainers, we want to help people, and we know this is best done when people value ongoing development. There's nothing worse then having to cram training down people's throats all day, every day. I am sure there are worse jobs, but it is certainly not fun.

As trainers, we can help our organizations build cultures of learning. Many factors shape a workplace's culture, but we can play a significant role in it. See the sidebar for tips on creating a culture of learning.

Does Your Organization Have a Culture of Learning?

Your workplace loves to learn if it meets these criteria:

✓ People are naturally curious and adventurous. The corporate environment encourages people to be curious and adventurous at work.

✓ People are allowed and encouraged to experiment. They strive to find new ways and approaches.

✓ The work environment is stimulating—sensual. The sights, sounds, smells, and textures are interesting and engaging.

✓ People at all levels seek and embrace learning in a variety of forms. (This is the most telling clue!) Employees have a high level of participation in learning events. (Note: If the problem is the training, this second indicator might not be accurate!)

✓ Management has a healthy view of failure and mistakes. Employees are held accountable, but productive recovery is also rewarded and mistakes are looked at as a learning experience.

✓ The workplace is intrinsically rewarding. When people are self-motivated, they seek more learning and development.

✓ The company proactively supports succession. People are developed and promoted.

✓ The company has a focus on innovation—in all functions and at all levels.

✓ The company embraces omnimodal learning and communication—in person, over the web, virtual, formal, informal, one-on-one, group, as part of regular meetings, as separate courses, on site, off site, and so on.

How does your work environment stack up? Management trainers can help build the conditions for a culture of learning by offering valued and engaging learning opportunities in a variety of ways that fit into managers' busy days. Being a learning role model is important, too. We need to practice what we preach and find ways to fit learning into our own busy schedules. I like the training Power Hours included in this manual because they are fun and help build a culture of learning.

Small = Big

If I were to summarize a theme for the management training included in this workbook, it would be that small equals big. As I mentioned in chapter 2, it is important to recognize that a manager's time is like platinum—very valuable and scarce. It is a big burden for managers to take a week off for training, and often they cannot concentrate on the training because of their operational concerns.

A great hour can be an amazing catalyst for learning. If done well, people think about the hour both before and after the training, and they are better able to apply the training to their everyday management situations. Power Hours can move mountains over time. I have offered 20 Power Hours here, but you can create hundreds more using the same general format. If you fully engage each manager once or twice per month for one hour, you *will* see shifts in managerial effectiveness and behavior.

Small really is big when the conversation is stimulating, and this should be your focus and goal. In fact, you can use 20- to 30-minute mini Power Hours and still do some great work!

Management Training Skills

As the engines for our organizations, managers deserve effective development that does not waste their precious time. Being a management trainer is important and rewarding work, and I applaud you for dedicating your time and energy to this endeavor. To be sure, being a management trainer is not for everyone, and everyone should not be a management trainer. When we hit a grand slam home run, we make a significant contribution to the organization. When we fail to deliver value for the time and resources we spend (ours and our learners'), however, an important opportunity is lost.

What does it take to be a great management trainer? I could create a list of 15 skills I think all trainers should have, but I don't think that would serve you well. You've heard of the 80/20 rule, right? The 80/20 rule states that the top 20 percent will produce 80 percent of the results. I think the 80/20 rule applies well to management training.

The 20 Percent That Will Get You 80 Percent

I believe that four characteristics or skills are most important to being an effective management trainer. I might cause a stir by suggesting these are the top four, but here goes:

1. Previous success as a manager

2. Business acumen

3. A passion and talent for being a catalyst

4. The ability to create and facilitate great dialogue.

Previous Success as a Manager

Do management trainers need to have management experience? I think they do, and they should have more than just experience. I think they also need to have been great managers. Management is a tough job and to help managers learn and grow, I think it is necessary to have done the work. For management trainers to garner trust, confidence, and influence with managers, they need to be able to relate to managers from a position of common ground.

Remember, I also suggest that management training should not be formal or rehearsed. If trainers could memorize the content and present it, then management experience would not be needed. At the foundation of the best management training, however, is the ability to create great business conversations, and I believe that the best people to facilitate these discussions are trainers who have done the work.

Here's one more thought that might not be popular: If you would not enjoy taking on the role of manager for two years (or more), then I question whether you should be a management trainer. I think management trainers should love management and enjoy being a manager. How will you be a powerful catalyst for managers if you find their jobs unappealing? If you don't want to be a manager, it will come through in your work.

The old saying goes something like this: Those who can't do, teach. Bunk! If you can't manage, and you don't want to learn to manage well, don't try training managers. I would recruit management trainers from the management ranks— recruit the very best and help them see the amazing contribution they could make by helping other managers excel.

Business Acumen

Management development is the art of helping managers manage a *business*. Everything about the training we provide managers is about business. We help managers understand their business, and we help them choose and develop practices that enable them to run their pieces of the business. Business, business, business. To be an effective management trainer, we need to know business.

The term *business acumen,* means knowledge of how the business runs—knowledge that helps us make good judgments and decisions. It is important that we are aware of our company's key indicators, its strategies, its target customers, and its market position. We should understand the key processes that managers use to run the business, such as budgeting, goal setting, forecasting, financial analysis, project implementation, hiring, and so on.

The good news is this: If you have management experience (and were successful at it), it is likely that you already possess business acumen. Management trainers without direct management experience need to ensure that they understand the business before they attempt to train managers. If you don't understand the business, it will be difficult to catalyze conversations, and your lack of skill will probably stand out like a three-piece suit at a Jimmy Buffet concert.

A Passion and Talent for Being a Catalyst

The first two characteristics of effective management trainers focus on background—the skills and experiences that will help them influence and develop managers. This characteristic is all about heart and motivation. I think it is critical that management trainers are driven to catalyze growth and development. This is not easy work and will require assertiveness, courage, and a deep reverence for the craft of management. Perhaps you are thinking that I am being a bit dramatic. Okay, I will admit that I may ride on the high side of passion for management development. Here's why: I have seen a lot of management training that made no difference, or made a negative impact, and seeing this waste drives me crazy. I am not being righteous. Earlier in my career, I delivered management training that I can see now was not a good use of the time, energy, and resources dedicated to it. I don't ever want to do that again, and I hope nothing but success for you. Every management trainer I have met has been smart, hardworking, and well meaning—every one. If we are going to pour ourselves into our work, let's make it count. Let's be catalysts for management transformation!

What does it take to be a catalyst? I propose that you practice four ways of being catalytic:

1. Be proactive.

2. Be curious.

3. Be courageous.

4. Be observant.

The bottom line is to be more in tune with what's needed for each situation—to do what will best enable the transformation. Honing my abilities to be a catalyst is a lifelong pursuit of mine, and I would love nothing more than to help you develop your catalyst's muscles, as well.

Be Proactive

It's tough to be a catalyst if you are not proactive. Being proactive is the first way of being for training catalysts. Listen and respond to what people are saying—and to what they obviously are *not* saying. Challenge managers, both intellectually and with regard to their intrinsic motivation, by stepping the conversation up to the next level of intimacy, complexity, or controversy. Take the initiative to offer learning solutions for today's business problems: Offer now the training that's needed now. Don't take months to support today's need. Take the initiative to get the right people together in conversation. Do whatever it takes to get people involved in the learning process.

Be Curious

The second way of being for catalysts is to be curious. Catalysts are often naturally curious people (as are trainers, right?). The more you encourage your curiosity, the more likely it is that you will be able to catalyze transformation. I see a strong connection between curiosity and learning because learning happens in layers. The outer layer is the surface. That's the kind of learning that occurs in any training session. As we go deeper, learning becomes much more personal and connective—connecting to work, interests, problems, and passions. Curiosity is often the vehicle we use to go deeper. We keep hiking, because we are curious about what's around the next bend. We keep listening because we are curious about where the conversation is headed. We ask more questions because we are curious about what someone will say. Let your curiosity flourish. Ask open-ended questions about what things mean and how they operate. Take an interest in understanding why and how things work.

Be Courageous

This next way of being—being courageous—is the one I see the least. Great trainers are very courageous people. They have to be, because that's how we make the greatest difference. This is where we can and should lead. Courage plays a big part in creating great dialogue because often it's what's *not* being said that *needs* to be said. Do you let training discussions ride on the surface, or do you ask that one question—the tough question—that will turn the conversation upside down and get everyone nervously engaged? I've never known or heard of a situation where a trainer was fired for being courageous. Having courage is not really risky, but you might find it uncomfortable or scary. Tension is not always a bad thing, though—it means that people are thinking and feeling. As long as you can get the conversation moving forward, putting a little tension in the room by bringing up what's on everyone's minds and no one's lips can be a great catalyst. Help training participants be more inclusive and authentic.

Be Observant
The final important way of being a good catalyst is to be observant. To be a great catalyst, you have to notice what's going on. Keep up with what's happening in the business and in each department. Notice the topics and behaviors (and perhaps people) that tend to engage or disengage training participants. Notice the major obstacles within the organization and enable your training to help obliterate managers' productivity barriers. Share your observations in ways that stimulate input and participation.

It's fun to be a positive catalyst. Most of us get into the field of training because we like to see the light bulbs come on over people's heads when they have that "ah-ha" moment. Catalysts create "ah-ha" moments every day.

The Ability to Create and Facilitate Great Dialogue

Trainers need to be able to generate and facilitate great business conversations. I wrote about the importance of this skill as it relates to coaching in *Coaching Basics*, also offered by the ASTD Press. The point is the same for coaching and training—we need to inspire and catalyze great conversation. Here's the section on creating great dialogue from *Coaching Basics* (chapter 4), adapted for trainers. Reading this section will also help you facilitate Power Hour 12: Meetings That Rock! because it touches on some of the same information.

The conversation is exciting, fast paced, and intellectually stimulating. Everyone is smart and focused. People solve problems quickly and think on their feet. Do you wish you could experience a work environment this provocative? Some places of employment are like this, and, more often than not, the reason is because they hire the right people and foster productive and engaging dialogue. People are talking about topics that matter, and what they talk about matters to them.

Painters need to understand the nature and properties of oils and canvas. English teachers need to know about semi-colons and dangling participles. Training occurs in conversation, so trainers need to be master conversationalists. As a trainer, you have the opportunity to create great dialogue and help managers become master conversationalists. When your work improves the level of dialogue, your effect on the organization will go beyond the help you offer your training participants.

You know great dialogue when you experience it. The level of engagement and energy far outshines the average business talk. Participants are actively thinking, listening, and contributing. Here are some elements of great training dialogue:

Relevance	The topic of discussion is one that people care about. It makes a difference in their lives.
Inquiry	Questions that are being asked move the topic forward. These questions are both provocative and evocative.
Freedom	Participants feel free to share their ideas and thoughts, even those thoughts that are on the fringe. The conversation is open.

Connectedness	There is a sense of shared purpose or interest. The participants feel connected to one another. All or most of the participants are contributing.
Reception	Participants listen well, interpret the information, provide feedback, and reinforce contribution.
Empowerment	People feel as though they have some influence on the topic being discussed. Ideally, this would mean that each and every person has the opportunity to change the course of the dialogue, and, therefore, the resulting actions and results.
Play	The conversation is fun and full of energy. It has an energy to it that flows and can be playful.

Great dialogue will exhibit many or all of these characteristics. In a work environment where employees engage in lively dialogue, people will quickly solve problems and be better able to seize opportunities. As a coach, you can help create an environment that encourages effective dialogue by addressing each of these characteristics.

Ensure Relevance of the Dialogue

When you work with managers, you will want to focus on how the training material will help them meet their daily management challenges. If they are not engaged, then maybe the topic is not relevant enough or you are not approaching it in a way that appeals to them. If you ask the right provocative or evocative questions, you should be able to grab their attention.

Encourage Inquiry

Inquiry is at the core of coaching. Managers seek development because they want to explore and improve their effectiveness and learn more about their skills. Asking questions is a great way to jump-start inquiry. Inquiry involves several types of questions, and they are not all treated equally. The two most common are closed ended and open ended:

❖ Closed-ended questions ask for a short or one-word answer. For example, "Do you want to be successful?"

❖ Open-ended questions ask for a longer, individualized answer. For example, "What would you like to accomplish this year?"

To create effective inquiry, you need to look deeper than whether the question is closed- or open ended. Both types can be poor or excellent questions, although open-ended questions provoke more involvement on the part of the recipient. The two examples listed here are both poor questions. They are not interesting and are much too general.

There is another way to look at creating inquiry, one that focuses on the quality of the questions you ask. As a trainer, you want to make sure that your questions are either provocative or evocative.

❖ Provocative questions excite and stimulate conversation. For example, "What would happen if...?"

❖ Evocative questions pull in participants and help bring images to mind. For example, "What kind of work makes you feel most engaged and satisfied?"

Inquiry plays a significant role in learning. Select questions that move the topic forward and engage your training participants.

Socrates, a Greek philosopher, was well known for his provocative and evocative questions. Using Socratic questions can generate rich information that helps participants succeed. You can help managers develop critical thinking and creativity skills. Socratic questions enable trainers to create an intriguing and fruitful dialogue. Rather than offering opinions and advice, the Socratic Method uses thought-provoking questions to promote learning. A well-executed Socratic question stretches the mind and challenges widely held beliefs.

When it comes to training discussions, the more questions you ask, the better, but the questions need to be great ones. If you are comfortable sharing your opinions and ideas, your challenge will be to resist giving advice. Advice rarely improves inquiry. Advice may be helpful at times, but the most effective training will facilitate your trainees' thinking processes. To do this, try using Socratic questions.

Socratic questions are probing, and most are open ended. You can use them in any situation. Inquiry creates change. It is the cornerstone of training discussions because it helps participants think and solve problems creatively. Socratic questions will also help participants clarify what they understand and in which areas they need more information. Throughout your training discussion, these questions will bring to light new strategies and ideas. When you ask great questions, you create exciting dialogue that managers will find intrinsically motivating. Table 3.1 offers a list of Socratic questions.

Using Socratic questions to generate inquiry improves the ability of managers to remain objective by facilitating their self-discoveries. The questions also serve to expand the trainees' analyses of the situation and to increase the number and quality of possibilities they consider. Using Socratic questions increases the energy of the dialogue and improves your trainees' learning.

Encourage the Freedom to Participate Fully

The effectiveness of your training dialogue can be crippled if you and your participants do not feel comfortable about being open and candid with each other. In a small-group training situation, you will want to establish ground rules and manage participation, so everyone is heard and all topics are considered. You may need to be the one to bring up a sensitive topic first, to help break the ice for the rest of the group. Make sure you deal diplomatically with over-participators or comments that quash the group's creativity and engagement.

Ensure Connectedness

Trainers sometimes walk a fine line between being involved and objective, and being separated. Even so, you can be very connected

Table 3.1 ❖ Socratic Questions

Situation	Socratic Question
To clarify your clients' goals	How would you like the change to occur?
	Why do you want this change?
	What will things look like in a year if everything goes as planned?
	What are the consequences of not changing?
To clarify your clients' intents or motives	Why do you want this outcome?
	How will you benefit?
	Why is this change important?
	What gave you this idea?
	Who will benefit from this change?
To ensure your clients' goals are aligned for success	How does this help you achieve your goal?
	What does this mean to you?
	What do you already know about this approach?
	How does this change affect the other aspects of the organization?
To uncover your clients' basic assumptions	What other assumptions could also be valid?
	Why do you believe this change is needed?
	What does your peer/manager/team think about this situation?
	What would happen if...?
	Why do you think I asked you this question?
To discover if your clients have enough information	What generalizations have you made?
	How do you know that...?
	Why is this situation occurring?
	Have you seen a situation similar to this before?
	What verification is there to support your claim?
To help your clients see other points of view	What are the pros and cons of your approach?
	How is this similar to or different from the way you have approached this in the past?
	What would an opponent of the idea say?
	What would your customers say?
	How would your competitors approach this?

to your training participants in that you take ownership of enabling their effectiveness through your training. Show an interest in the progress; show them that their successes matter to you. Being connected means having a strong and deep relationship. As a trainer, you want to be connected in a way that recognizes and honors each of your roles.

Improve Dialogue Reception

Many things get in the way of dialogue reception. Miscommunication, censored feedback, and poor listening can wreck a conversation. You may not hear what managers are trying to tell you, even if you hear the words they are speaking. Communication between two people goes through each person's filters. Figure 3.1 shows how messages change as they pass through the filters (mindset, biases, and opinions) of both the sender and the receiver.

Trainers need to listen to the words that are being spoken and hear their clients' intentions, or disconnects will occur. Even with the best of intentions, messages can become distorted and confused. Trainers who learn to listen well and to provide effective feedback will improve overall dialogue reception.

Active and deep listening is a critical skill for trainers. Active listening is critical because so much of your work depends on clear communications and good relationships. It is a way of

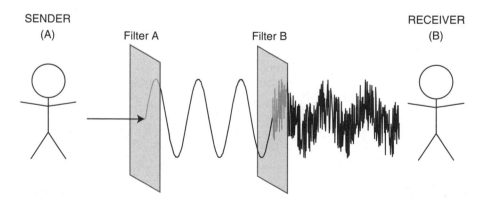

FIGURE 3.1 ❖ How messages change as they flow through senders' and receivers' individual filters.

listening and responding to managers that improves mutual understanding. Many people are poor listeners. They get distracted, talk too much, and think about what they are going to say next when they should be listening. They assume they know what other people are going to say and tune them out. It can be difficult to take the time and energy to listen actively, but the rewards are worth the effort. Here are some ways you can listen actively:

❖ Demonstrate a sincere desire to pay attention to the other person (instead of mentally practicing what you are going to say next).

❖ Commit to being coachable and open with the information you receive from the other person.

❖ Relate to the other person's perspective, and empathize.

❖ Seek to understand the other person.

❖ Pay attention, and resist being distracted by other things in the environment.

❖ Make sure that you have interpreted the message as intended through feedback, confirming, restating, or paraphrasing.

❖ Reflect on what the other person is saying.

❖ Synthesize the information, emotion, and feelings to improve understanding.

❖ Clarify the information by asking questions and probing.

❖ Validate perceptions and assumptions.

❖ Allow the other person to talk.

❖ Focus on the other person, and be fully present.

Many people let full calendars, long to-do lists, stress, and their natural behavioral tendencies get in the way of their ability to actively listen. To get in the habit of listening actively, try the tips listed in the sidebar.

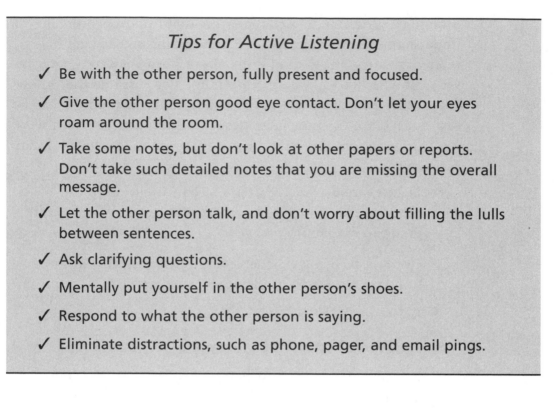

Tips for Active Listening

✓ Be with the other person, fully present and focused.

✓ Give the other person good eye contact. Don't let your eyes roam around the room.

✓ Take some notes, but don't look at other papers or reports. Don't take such detailed notes that you are missing the overall message.

✓ Let the other person talk, and don't worry about filling the lulls between sentences.

✓ Ask clarifying questions.

✓ Mentally put yourself in the other person's shoes.

✓ Respond to what the other person is saying.

✓ Eliminate distractions, such as phone, pager, and email pings.

Active listening is a habit that you can and must develop. Being a great listener benefits you as a trainer because it reduces misunderstandings, improves the accuracy of information shared, and ensures that trainees have complete information from which to work. Managers open up more to people who listen well.

Improve Topic Empowerment
When training conversations focus on the topics that are most important to managers, achieving topic empowerment is not generally a problem. If training participants do not feel as though they can make changes or use the suggested techniques, however, they may feel disconnected from the discussion. It is important that you help participants connect with the content and determine how it applies to their work, or they may tune out or become frustrated. Topic empowerment is important. We want managers to feel they can make a difference—because they can!

Keep Conversations Playful

You can do a lot to keep your training discussions playful. A playful conversation doesn't need to lack seriousness. In this context, playfulness means playing with ideas, concepts, and information such that the conversation's energy level is high. Here are several ways you can improve conversation playfulness:

1. Ask participants to read interesting and provocative articles before the training.

2. Change the context of the training session to a place that is intellectually stimulating.

3. Diagram, or chart out (e.g.,"mind-map") the conversation.

4. Share a success story of someone with a similar goal.

5. Use idea-generation techniques.

6. Plan the agenda of the training session so the meeting moves quickly and flows well. Begin with an attention grabber, and try to plan for a high point toward the end of the meeting.

7. Give unconventional and intriguing homework assignments. For example, ask participants to contact their role models. Suggest that they change one behavior for one week. Suggest a thought-provoking movie or live performance that relates to the topic under discussion.

To make conversations more playful, you want to have a variety of contexts and types of information coming together. Tap into the interests and needs of your clients, and offer information that will stretch and broaden their perspectives.

Training is more of an art than a science. It is a dialogue that you drive and keep focused on the learners. Effective training produces energy. Whether participants leave your training sessions with more energy and excitement depends on the quality of the dialogue. Great dialogue is stimulating, intriguing, and enlightening, and the best trainers make this happen in a seamless and almost magical way.

As I wrote at the beginning of this chapter, I could list a bunch of skills that will help you be a great management trainer.

Many qualities are useful—organization, sense of urgency, public speaking prowess, and consultation skills are just a few. That said, I honestly believe that if you have been a successful manager, have business acumen, possess a passion for being a learning catalyst, and can facilitate great conversations, you have the ingredients necessary to be a great management trainer.

What to Do Next

❖ Determine if your workplace has a culture of learning. Do a self-assessment and discuss it with your manager and peers. Find ways to improve the culture.

❖ Begin to see and capitalize on opportunities to provide training in tiny increments.

❖ Determine how *you* need to develop to become a better management trainer. Create your own learning plan and implement it!

CHAPTER 4

Using Training Power Hours

What's Covered in This Chapter

- ❖ Topics in this collection of Power Hours
- ❖ Suggestions for scheduling and pairing Power Hours
- ❖ Alternative styles of delivery
- ❖ Training they don't know they're getting
- ❖ Key Dos and Don'ts for using the Management Training Power Hours

Power Hour Topics

This collection of Management Training Power Hours does not make for a complete curriculum of management training. To be complete, the manual would need to contain hundreds of Power Hours! The manager's job is complex and always changing. The 20 Power Hours included in this book address fundamental and enduring topics that touch on several common challenges:

✓ Job perception

✓ Expectations

✓ Time management

✓ Team development.

Several Power Hours address each topic. On the other hand, by design, the Power Hours in this manual do not cover certain managerial activities:

❖ Recruiting

❖ Counseling and termination

❖ Performance appraisal

❖ Change management

❖ Facilitation

❖ Project management

❖ Self-development.

I did not touch on performance appraisals, counseling and termination, or recruiting because companies often have very specific procedures for these functions. For example, I did not offer a Power Hour about change management because this is a topic best covered with a specific change in mind, and the content should be specific to the situation (in addition, addressing it might take more than an hour). I encourage you to create your own collection of Power Hours to best suit the needs of your managers.

My favorite Power Hours are 4: Your Management A-B Boxes, 5: Your Management-Filter, and 7: Grand Slam Home Runs. If you present these three Power Hours over and over until everyone has participated, you will have spent your time wisely.

Suggestions for Scheduling and Pairing Power Hours

I realize that the format of 20 one-hour sessions is not traditional. I encourage you to *not* clump seven of these into a daylong training session. I think management training is best done in small bites and repeatedly, so that's the format I have offered. There are a few Power Hours that make for good pairings if you want to do two in a month, or a series of two or three at a time (one per week for three weeks). Here's how I would match them up:

Set 1:	1: Management in the Modern Times, 2: What's Expected of You, 3: Managing and Improving Your Reputation, 4: Your Management A-B Boxes
Set 2:	4: Your Management A-B Boxes, 5: Your Management Filter, 11: Results-Oriented Responses, 15: Your Leadership Legacy
Set 3:	6: Mind Your Metrics! 7: Grand Slam Home Runs, 8: Defining Excellence, 9: Communicating Expectations
Set 4:	10: The Art of Planning, 12: Meetings That Rock! 13: Mastering Your Time
Set 5:	14: Internal Service Excellence, 16: Knowing When and How to Say "No," 17: Aligning Your Department for Success
Set 6:	18: The Art of Employee One-on-Ones, 19: Enlivening Minds at Work, 20: Encouraging Collaboration

To make it more convenient for managers to attend, present each Power Hour at a variety of different times and days of the week. We need to carry the burden of making it easy for the managers to engage in the learning. No matter how crazy our days are, it is likely that most managers are dealing with more competing demands and pressure.

Alternative Styles of Delivery

I encourage you to be creative about how you bring these Management Training Power Hours to your organization. You will notice that they are low-tech—no fancy equipment or Power Point projectors are needed. This allows you to focus on the quality of the conversation and to deliver the Power Hours under varying conditions.

Does the management team meet regularly for staff meetings? If so, negotiate for one hour per month to deliver a Power Hour during a staff meeting. It's a great way to link to whatever is already happening. If the staff meeting lasts two hours, request the first hour, so you don't get bumped when topics run overtime—and make sure you never run overtime, either.

I like delivering the Power Hours within intact management teams on a regular basis, such as once every two weeks. This allows for follow-up on homework and creates continuity of conversation. You can see the light bulbs going off during each session and hear how each manager is applying what he or she learns.

You can present the Power Hours in a virtual conversation, but this situation is not optimal because it is hard to have a vigorous conversation on a conference call. A videoconference setup is better. I encourage you to offer the prework using online tools (emailing, podcasting, and webcasting).

I have also delivered Power Hours as brown-bag-lunch meetings. People bring their PB&Js and chat while eating. This is a perfectly fine method if it helps managers get the training. Try a 5:00 p.m. pizza chat or an 8:00 a.m. donut chat—whatever gets people engaged.

Training They Don't Know They're Getting

My favorite kind of management training is not acknowledged, measured, or scheduled. How is that possible? I love training that is covert—people learn but they don't even know they are being trained. Woohoo! Management trainers can be, and should be, good at developing managers without the managers even realizing what's happening. They know *something* is happening, but they aren't likely to call it training. Their projects are more on track, they are enjoying greater focus, and meetings are more productive. Where does this stealthy learning occur? Everywhere! When does it happen? All the time!

Let's infuse our work environments with provocative and evocative information about the state of the art in management. Offer training on bulletin boards, during staff meetings, during project planning, on internal blogs, and during informal business discussions. Little bits here and there will add up and make a big difference. If we really believe that continuous learning is an important part of every job, then let's model this by making learning happen everywhere and in many ways.

Use the Power Hours for inspiration and focus. If you plan to offer Power Hour 10: The Art of Planning, this month, saturate the physical and virtual work environment with great information about planning, including tips, success stories, the potential pitfalls of poor planning, interesting articles, and blog posts. At each management staff meeting that you facilitate, ask open-ended questions about planning that evoke reflection on current practices and needs.

How to Succeed Using the Management Training Power Hours

I hope you give the Management Training Power Hours a try in your organization! These training chats will help you engage managers in meaningful conversations about their craft. See the sidebar for a few Dos and Don'ts that will help you succeed in using these materials.

Enjoy being a facilitator of these amazing conversations and relish your role as a learning catalyst!

Key Dos and Don'ts for Using Management Training Power Hours

❖ Do offer the Power Hours multiple times and often.

❖ Do keep the time to an hour. Time is precious, and you want to build a reputation for sticking to the agenda.

❖ Do have fun with these modules! Add your own examples and flair.

❖ Do send out the prework—always. Take some time to find a short but provocative piece to get managers thinking. Even if they skip out on the training, they might learn something from the prework!

❖ Don't clump the Power Hours together. They are meant to be presented one at a time. Respect your managers' time.

❖ Don't build a PowerPoint presentation for the Power Hours. Focus on the conversation, not the presentation.

❖ Don't take "No" for an answer. Continue to offer learning in a variety of ways until you begin to build a following for this brand of applied informal learning.

What to Do Next

❖ Test one of the Power Hours with your peer team. Play with it and see how it fits your style.

❖ Schedule a couple of Power Hours and get started! Go deep and immerse the work environment with subtle bits of great information.

CHAPTER 5

Make Sure Time Is Well Spent

What's Covered in This Chapter

- ❖ Ensuring that development time is well spent
- ❖ Measuring the value of management training
- ❖ Evaluating the focus of your course offerings

Ensuring That Development Time Is Well Spent

Remember management training theory (MTT) from chapter 2? A manager's time is precious. I believe that determining if our training time is time well spent is a fundamental responsibility, and sometimes this is not done adequately. It is not good enough to demonstrate that our training programs have some positive value. We need to show that spending time in training is a great use of time relative to all the other possible ways in which managers spend their time. What are the opportunity costs? (These are the costs associated with *not* spending time doing a different task.) Do the training expenditures still make sense after these costs are factored in? When managers leave your training classes, do they feel as though the training gained was well worth the disruption to their schedule and their routine?

If we start off with this higher-value hurdle in mind, we will better plan and select our training programs. The challenge is determining whether something is a great use of time, and that process is subjective. In fact, some of the best training sessions might leave participants feeling some sort of dissonance or frustration. That said, I tend to use the criteria listed in the sidebar to get a rough feel for whether training time is spent wisely.

The more you can answer "Yes" to the questions in the sidebar, the more likely it is that the time the managers spent training was time well spent. I am not a big fan of smile sheets—those evaluation forms passed out at the end of a training session—but it is useful to get written feedback from managers from time

Was Training Time Well Spent?

1. Was this a great conversation about the business?

2. Were participants engaged in the discussion?

3. Was the topic aligned to the strategies? In other words, will the topic help managers get their jobs done more effectively?

4. Was the session as short as it could be (and still a great conversation)? Did it respect people's time?

5. Did the participants leave with a clear idea of what they should do next to apply this learning? Did they have homework? Do managers do the homework?

6. Do managers attend the sessions willingly and voluntarily?

to time. The key question to ask is, "Do you consider our training programs to be a great use of your precious time? Why or why not?"

Measuring the Value of Management Training

Ensuring that training time is spent wisely is just the beginning. We have a broader and more important purpose we need to fulfill: Does management training improve management performance? Many great books and training programs can teach you how to measure and improve training return on investment (ROI). When it comes to management training, though, I like to focus on measuring my impact on business results based on the results that managers are expected to achieve. Each business is different, but the most common expectation for managers is that they attain several goals:

- ✓ They complete projects on time, on budget, and to an acceptable quality.

- ✓ They meet financial targets, including revenue generation, cost management, and profitability.

- ✓ They maintain and develop a talented team and reduce negative (unwanted) turnover.

- ✓ They ensure that work processes and schedules are effective and efficient.

These are the basics. Then, some companies might ask managers to deliver results based on innovation, product development, compliance, or other business metrics. These results can and should be measured to ensure that the management function is working.

The difficulty with using business metrics to measure training performance is that it can be difficult to isolate the impact of the training compared to all the other business improvement initiatives that might be occurring at the same time. To meet this challenge, I offer one idea and one suggestion. Here's the idea, by way of a story. When I worked for Black & Decker, I supported their network of more than 100 service centers across the United States. These were the freestanding stores into which we would go to buy Black & Decker products or get our drills and lawn mowers fixed. Each store had a manager, who was held responsible for productivity, safety, and profitability. My first major project with this division was to create a manager training program called Service University. The program consisted of a week of training held at the division's headquarters in Maryland. Twelve at a time, the managers would come to Service University. The overall goal for the program was to improve manager performance as well as service center performance.

I measured the impact of the system by tracking three sets of data. First, I documented the benchmark levels of performance for all service centers in terms of key metrics (profit, budget, and turnover). Then, six months after attending Service University, I noted each manager's performance in terms of these same metrics. I compared the improvements to the average improvements achieved by managers who had not yet attended Service University. I was able to document that managers who attended Service University improved their business metrics by 5 percent more than those who had not attended.

That was over 20 years ago, and there are many things I would do differently if I were to have the same assignment. One thing I would not change, however, is the way I approached measuring success. The focus on service center metrics facilitated two important catalysts for success: First, when I was able to demonstrate real business results, I never (never!) had to fight for funding or the time of service center managers. Second, because I set the training system up to focus on results, I tuned my team and myself to make better and more focused choices about the training content and design.

When you are working with a large group of managers across all functions, it can be a bit more difficult to focus on results and to isolate the impact of your training. To address this challenge, here is a suggestion I made earlier: Get over it, and do it anyway! I am not advocating that you establish an elaborate process for tracking training attendee performance metrics. If you were to do this, you'd spend more time and money measuring training than you would providing training (this is my major beef with many training ROI processes). You can, however, create a simple dashboard that tracks basic management deliverables.

Evaluating the Focus of Your Course Offerings: A Quick Test

What should your management training dashboard look like? It depends on your business, but several fundamental metrics will apply in many companies. To ensure your focus on both training conversation quality and overall results, I recommend creating a dashboard with two parts. Worksheet 5.1 offers an example you can use and modify to fit your particular needs.

You can use common sense for some of these measures, but be mindful of ways to improve data quality. For example, I would tend to ask the finance department to rate performance to budget, not department leaders. For this measure, I would sit with a financial analyst (or whoever works with managers on budget matters), go through the list of managers one by one, and ask those managers if they are currently managing the department—in terms of costs, revenues (if applicable), and profits—as planned in the budget or forecast. Bob Smith, "Yes" or "No"; Liz Green, "Yes" or "No"; Todd Knight, "Yes" or "No." Get a "Yes" or "No" for each manager every three months. Then you can track the changes in performance. If you asked a general question, such as "What percentage of managers are managing within budget?" you would not get an accurate reading. You might be thinking, "Yeah, but what if other business issues are causing the financial problems? I don't want to get dinged for something that is out of my control."

I don't worry about these things. I want to improve management capability and results, especially if the business is struggling. I think senior leaders will know to factor in outside influences when reviewing the data. The data is still important and should affect your training offerings. For example, if the data shows that performance to budget is getting worse (for whatever

Worksheet 5.1

Management Training Dashboard

Use this dashboard to track and measure the effectiveness and value of your management training. Add and replace metrics based on your company's current goals and priorities.

Part 1—Management Function Metrics

Metric	Baseline	+ 3 Months	+ 6 Months	+12 Months
Project completion—timely				
Project completion—budget				
Project completion—quality				
Performance to budget				
Negative turnover				

Part 2—Training Session Quality

Metric	Baseline	+ 3 Months	+ 6 Months	+12 Months
Quality of conversations				
Focused topics				
Managers feel training is a great use of time				
Managers do the homework				
Respects managers' time				
Managers seek to attend				

reason), I would want to pay more attention to this area in my training. If the challenge is new competition or a market shift, how can I help managers respond to this challenge?

You will notice that I have not included a lot of the less-results-driven metrics that might be found on a manager's performance evaluation. I prefer to focus on business results, not on issues such as whether managers get their performance evaluations done on time or turn in perfect paperwork. Resist the temptation (or requests from HR) to measure your training effectiveness by these indirect measures, because they will not tell you whether you are improving management results.

If I were leading a management training function for a company, I would want to have the information found using this dashboard. Management training is an ongoing function, so it doesn't matter where you start your baseline measurements because your goal is always to help managers improve.

What to Do Next

- ❖ Create a training dashboard using Worksheet 5.1 as a starting point.

- ❖ Share the dashboard with a group of managers and get their input on how to use the data to better shape training efforts.

PART II
The Power Hours

CHAPTER 6

Introducing 20 POWER HOUR Manager Training Sessions

What's Covered in This Chapter

❖ Index to the Power Hours

❖ Structure of the Power Hours

Index to the Power Hours

Here are the Power Hours included in this book:
1: Management in the Modern Times—chapter 7, p. 59
2: What's Expected of You—chapter 8, p. 65

Structure of the Power Hours

All the Power Hours are structured in the same way for two reasons:

1. To make it easier on you, the trainer. Once you have presented one or two of the Power Hours, you will be able to quickly prepare and deliver all of them.

2. To make it easier for the participants. The trainees need to become accustomed to this type of learning experience, because they get the most out of it when they come prepared and participate.

Without this structure—and the active dialogue it facilitates—your Power Hour would be a Power 30 Minutes. Next, we'll review the elements in the facilitator's guide for each Power Hour.

Prework Assignment

I like to get managers thinking and talking about a topic before the training session. The prework is meant to be a warm-up, not a preview of the content. My favorite prereading assignments come from weblog (blog) posts or podcasts (audio). There are many smart and well-written blogs that focus on management and leadership. Blog posts tend to be short, interesting, and provocative—perfect elements for prereading. Podcasts can be an interesting and engaging way to get managers talking. You can email managers with the link to the podcasts, and they can listen from their computer or download the podcast onto their iPod or other MP3 player. Articles or portions of books also make great prereading.

I think it is important that you select your own prereading materials. Each piece should be relevant and interesting to your audience. If you don't read blogs or listen to podcasts currently, see the sidebar for a good starter list with which management trainers ought to be familiar. They will offer a lot of options for prework assignments.

Starter List of Blogs

Blogs can be an important source of your Power Hour prereading assignments. Here's a starter list. Hot links are provided on the CD.

My blog—Management Craft: www.managementcraft.com

My podcasts: www.lisahaneberg.com/podcasts-and-webcasts/

800*ceoread* Blog: www.800ceoread.com/blog/

Agile Management Blog: www.agilemanagement.net/Articles/Weblog/blog.html

BusinessPundit: www.businesspundit.com

David Lorenzo: www.careerintensity.com/blog/

Come Gather Round: www.ongenius.com/blog/

Cranky Middle Manager: http://cmm.thepodcastnetwork.com/

Fast Company's blog http://blog.fastcompany.com/

Genuine Curiosity: www.genuinecuriosity.com/genuinecuriosity/

Johnnie Moore's blog: www.johnniemoore.com/blog/

Management-Issues: www.management-issues.com/default.asp

Management Skills Blog: www.managementblog.org/

Manager Tools: www.manager-tools.com/

Make It Great With Phil Gerbyshak: www.makeitgreat.typepad.com/makeitgreat/

Ramblings From a Glass Half Full: www.tshalffull.blogspot.com/

Seth Godin's Blog: www.sethgodin.typepad.com/seths_blog/

Slacker Manager: www.slackermanager.com/

Slow Leadership: www.slowleadership.org/blog/

Talking Story With Say Leadership Coaching: www.sayleadershipcoaching.com/talkingstory/

You Already Know This Stuff: www.youalreadyknowthisstuff.blogspot.com/

Learning Objectives

The learning objectives for the Power Hour training sessions are simple. With this type of training, we want managers to reflect on the topic, reflect on their current management practices, determine how the topic relates to their goals, and make small adjustments to the way they manage. Some Power Hours have specific homework assignments that ask managers to apply suggested techniques, whereas others call for a change in mindset.

Trainer's Objective

Your overall objective for all Power Hours is to produce a one-hour training session that catalyzes great conversations between managers about management. This, to me, is the most important objective of all. When managers are engaged in discussing their craft, they will learn more and try new approaches more readily.

Agenda

You will notice that the Power Hours all have a consistent rhythm, or agenda, and this is by design. We want people to know what to expect, like we do when we walk into a McDonald's Restaurant in Paris, France. A Big Mac is a Big Mac. A Power Hour is a Power Hour. Here is the basic agenda for most of the sessions:

10 Minutes	Brief discussion of prework (and homework if you are doing these in a series; see chapter 4). Pass out the handout.
15 Minutes	Presentation of the conceptual model or topic
10 Minutes	Initial discussion of the concept
15 Minutes	Exercise/application
10 Minutes	Final discussion and assignment of homework

Power Hours are named such because they move very quickly —they are packed with power and energy. The agenda ensures that this is the case. It is important to keep the group sizes small so that the discussion does not take longer than the time allotted. If you want to increase the group size and lengthen the session, you can do so, but it won't feel quite as invigorating.

Provo/Evo Discussion Questions

For each Power Hour, I offer several provocative and evocative (provo/evo) questions that you can use to facilitate a discussion of the topic. I would encourage you to create your own provo/evo questions, as well—perhaps those that you yourself wonder about. It's wonderful when trainers are obviously interested in the topics they train, so I would encourage you to add your own questions to the discussion.

Conceptual Model

Each Power Hour highlights a topic or focuses on a concept. The conceptual model is simply the topic being discussed, with a paragraph or two of information and perhaps a model or graphic to get the discussion going. Feel free to change or add to this portion of the Power Hour, as long as it does not affect the overall timing. Keeping the session to one hour is important.

Exercise

You will ask managers to process the topic by doing an exercise. Sometimes the exercise is done in groups or pairs, and sometimes it is done individually. The important fact about Power Hour exercise topics, however, is that they all relate directly to the managers' jobs.

Homework/Application Assignment

If you offer the Power Hours in an ad-hoc manner, the homework relies on the honor system. If you are doing a series of Power Hours with the same group, you can discuss the homework at the beginning of the next session. Either way, I think it is important to assign the homework. Like the exercise, the homework relates directly to managers' jobs and presumably will help make their work easier and more fruitful. You always want to suggest that people do something with their key learnings.

The homework assignments are simple. They serve to put the topics discussed into action. Focused action leads to better results.

Power Hour Handout

Each Power Hour has a corresponding one-page handout. There are no other training materials for the participant, except the pre-reading assignment. The handout is sometimes two sided, and if it is, please do copy the two pages back to back. Participants make a psychological distinction between a one-page handout and one that is stapled. The Power Hour should always take one hour and should always come with one piece of paper as a hand-out—this is part of the feel and magic of this ongoing type of management training. There are no big training binders collect-ing dust!

CHAPTER 7

POWER HOUR 1:
Management in
the Modern Times

Prework Assignment

Find a brief, current article or blog post to share with people as a warm-up to this Power Hour. It's OK, and preferred, for the piece to be provocative or controversial. The prework should stir conversation and prime people for an exploration of the topic.

Learning Objectives

While completing this Power Hour and the application homework, participants will

1. Discuss today's unique and complex nature of managing

2. Identify key enablers and barriers to their productivity, such that they can address and optimize them

3. Create a plan to reduce one or more barriers in the coming week.

Trainer's Objective

The trainer will produce a one-hour training session that catalyzes great conversations between managers about management.

Agenda

10 Minutes	Brief discussion of prework (and homework if you are doing the Power Hours in a series; see chapter 4). Pass out the handout.
15 Minutes	Presentation of the conceptual model or topic
10 Minutes	Initial discussion of the concept using provo/evo questions
15 Minutes	Exercise/application
10 Minutes	Final discussion and assignment of homework

Provo/Evo Discussion Questions

1. Why do you manage?

2. Does the complexity of your day make your job more or less interesting and appealing to you?

3. What will the future likely bring? Will management become more or less complex and difficult?

4. If managers are the organization's engines, what practices will best help the engine run well and strong?

5. What can managers do to improve the efficiency and importance of the inputs to their funnels?

Conceptual Model

Management is a craft—developed and built over time and with great care. Great managers link goals with results and facilitate the flow of work. They are the "get-it-done" people. They can make a significant positive impact on business results. Being a manager is challenging: Managers deal with ever-changing demands, ambiguous priorities, barriers, breakdowns, and a full range of human emotions. Great managers are gifted in many ways and disciplines.

In Figure 7.1, management is represented by the funnel. Inputs and requests from senior management and administrative support groups such as accounting and human resources come into the funnel and demand time, care, and resources. Managers need to sort out these various requests and create a work plan for their teams. Sometimes, the number of inputs entering the funnel is in excess of the manager's and his or her team's capacity to execute them. Barriers, or "Mucky Muck," can get in the way of the smooth execution of work.

Managers and therefore trainers have one premise: To optimize management effectiveness—and thereby team effectiveness and business results—you need to ensure that the inputs are focused and efficient, while removing as much Mucky Muck as possible.

FIGURE 7.1 ❖ The management funnel.

Exercise

Split the group into two smaller groups. Give each team 10 minutes to generate a list of responses to the these questions:

Group 1   Brainstorm 10 ways you can help improve the efficiency and quality of the inputs coming into your management funnel.

Group 2   Brainstorm the five most common barriers to your productivity and 10 ways you can reduce or eliminate these barriers.

Homework/Application Assignment

Select two or three ideas from the exercise to implement or work on over the next week.

POWER HOUR 1 Handout ❖ Management in the Modern Times

Management is a craft—developed and built over time and with great care. Great managers link goals with results and facilitate the flow of work. They are the get-it-done people, and they can make a significant positive impact on business results. Being a manager is challenging. Managers deal with ever-changing demands, ambiguous priorities, barriers, breakdowns, and a full range of human emotions. Great managers are gifted in many ways and disciplines.

Management is represented by the funnel. Inputs and requests from senior management and administrative support groups such as accounting and human resources come into the funnel and demand time, care, and resources. Managers need to sort out these various requests and create a work plan for their teams. Sometimes the number of inputs entering the funnel is in excess of the capacity of the manager and his or her team to execute them. In addition, barriers, or Mucky Muck, can get in the way of a smooth execution of work.

POWER HOUR 1 Handout ❖ Management in the Modern Times

Premise: To optimize management effectiveness—and thereby team effectiveness and business results—you need to ensure that the inputs are focused and efficient while removing as much Mucky Muck as possible.

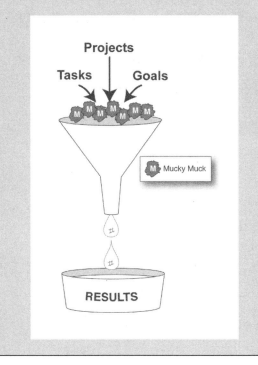

CHAPTER 8

 # POWER HOUR 2:
What's Expected
of You

Prework Assignment

Find a brief, current article or blog post to share with people as a warm-up to this Power Hour. It's OK, and preferred, for the piece to be provocative or controversial. The prework should stir conversation and prime people for an exploration of the topic.

Learning Objectives

While completing this Power Hour and the application home-work, participants will

1. Discuss the importance of understanding expectations and their manager's definition of excellence

2. Identify questions they can ask their manager and peers to define their expectations

3. Create a plan to conduct a one-on-one session to clarify expectations with their manager in the coming week.

Trainer's Objective

The trainer will produce a one-hour training session that catalyzes great conversations between managers about management.

Agenda

10 Minutes	Brief discussion of prework (and homework if you are presenting these in a series; see chapter 4). Pass out the handout.
15 Minutes	Presentation of the conceptual model or topic
10 Minutes	Initial discussion of the concept using provo/evo questions
15 Minutes	Exercise/application
10 Minutes	Final discussion and assignment of homework

Provo/Evo Discussion Questions

1. Do you know what's expected of you with regard to how you manage and improve the capacity of your department? With regard to who you are as a manager and leader?

2. Do you know how your manager would define *excellence*? If so, does this differ from your definition?

3. What clues might indicate what your managers value most?

4. When was the last time you asked your manager what he or she thought the organization needed from you most? How do you think your manager would respond to this question?

Conceptual Model

Many managers do not know what's expected of them beyond a list of projects and tasks to be completed on time and within budget. Expectations go much deeper than this, though, and it is both important and valuable to know how your manager defines excellent performance. You will have a much better chance of meeting and exceeding expectations if you understand what excellence looks like in the eyes of your managers and peers.

Table 8.1 lists some questions you can ask your manager that will help you determine expectations. This list of questions might seem daunting, but each one affects your manager's overall expectations and his or her impressions of your current performance.

Table 8.1 ❖ Questions to Ask to Help Determine Expectations

Topic Area	Question
Basic Job Function	1. How do you define *quality of work*? 2. What are your expectations regarding deadlines and communication of work status? 3. What does "being prepared" mean?
Decision Making	1. What is your expectation of me with regard to making and communicating decisions? 2. What types of decisions would you like to join me in making?
Work Environment	1. Describe the work environment you expect me to build and reinforce. 2. In what ways would you like to see the company's culture change, and what role do you believe I should play in creating that transformation? 3. Is there anything about the department's current culture that you think should change or improve?
Creativity and Innovation	1. Describe what it means to be creative. 2. How important are creativity and innovation, and what are your expectations of me with regard to them?

(continued)

Table 8.1 ❖ Questions to Ask to Help Determine Expectations

	3. In what ways would you like me and my group to generate new ideas and improve results?
Team Development and Productivity	1. Describe for me your vision of how a well-functioning team looks and feels?
	2. What expectations do you have of me with regard to team development and productivity?
	3. How would you like me to manage and correct poor performance?
	4. How much time do you think I should spend coaching others?
Communication	1. What does effective communication look like in your eyes?
	2. What are your expectations of me with regard to communication?
	3. What are your expectations of me with regard to attending and conducting meetings?
Growth and Development	1. Everyone needs to continue to grow. In what two ways would you most like to see me grow and develop over the next year?
Results Orientation	1. What does it mean to be results oriented?
	2. What are your expectations of me with regard to getting results and being results oriented?
Partnership	1. How important is partnership and collaboration?
	2. What are your expectations of me with regard to our level of partnership and collaboration?
	3. In what ways would you like to see partnership and collaboration improve?
Ethics and Role Modeling	1. What does it mean to represent the company well?
	2. What are your expectations for how managers should conduct themselves and represent the company?

(continued)

Exercise

Using Table 8.1, create an interview plan on the back of your handout with the 10 questions you would most like to ask your manager to better understand his or her expectations.

Homework/Application Assignment

Schedule and complete a one-on-one meeting with your manager in the next week. Use your interview plan as a guide for this meeting.

POWER HOUR 2 Handout ❖ What's Expected of You

Many managers do not know what's expected of them beyond a list of projects and tasks to be completed on time and within budget. Expectations go much deeper than that, however, and it is important and valuable to know how your manager defines excellent performance. You will have a much better chance of meeting and exceeding expectations if you understand what excellence looks like in the eyes of your managers and peers.

Here are some questions you can ask that will help you determine expectations.

Topic Area	Question
Basic Job Function	1. How do you define *quality of work*?
	2. What are your expectations regarding deadlines and communication of work status?
	3. What does "being prepared" mean?
Decision Making	1. What is your expectation of me with regard to making and communicating decisions?
	2. What types of decisions would you like to join me in making?

(continued)

POWER HOUR 2 Handout ❖ What's Expected of You

Work Environment	1. Describe the work environment you expect me to build and reinforce.
	2. In what ways would you like to see the company's culture change, and what role do you believe I should play in creating that transformation?
	3. Is there anything about the department's current culture that you think should change or improve?
Creativity and Innovation	1. Describe what it means to be creative.
	2. How important are creativity and innovation, and what are your expectations of me with regard to them?
	3. In what ways would you like me and my group to generate new ideas and improve results?
Team Development and Productivity	1. Describe for me your vision of how a well-functioning team looks and feels?
	2. What expectations do you have of me with regard to team development and productivity?
	3. How would you like me to manage and correct poor performance?
	4. How much time do you think I should spend coaching others?
Communication	1. What does effective communication look like in your eyes?
	2. What are your expectations of me with regard to communication?
	3. What are your expectations of me with regard to attending and conducting meetings?

(continued)

70

POWER HOUR 2 Handout ❖ What's Expected of You

Growth and Development	1. Everyone needs to continue to grow. In what two ways would you most like to see me grow and develop over the next year?
Results Orientation	1. What does it mean to be results oriented? 2. What are your expectations of me with regard to getting results and being results oriented?
Partnership	1. How important is partnership and collaboration? 2. What are your expectations of me with regard to our level of partnership and collaboration? 3. In what ways would you like to see partnership and collaboration improve?
Ethics and Role Modeling	1. What does it mean to represent the company well? 2. What are your expectations for how managers should conduct themselves and represent the company?

Expectations One-on-One—Interview Plan

List the questions you will ask during the one-on-one with your manager.

_____

_____

_____

_____

_____

_____

_____

_____

_____

_____

CHAPTER 9

POWER HOUR 3: Managing and Improving Your Reputation

Prework Assignment

Find a brief, current article or blog post to share with people as a warm-up to this Power Hour. It's OK, and preferred, for the piece to be provocative or controversial. The prework should stir conversation and prime people for an exploration of the topic.

Learning Objectives

While completing this Power Hour and the application homework, participants will

1. Discuss the importance of knowing their managerial reputation

2. Self-assess their managerial reputation

3. Collect feedback about their reputation from managers and peers.

Trainer's Objective

The trainer will produce a one-hour training session that catalyzes great conversations between managers about management.

Agenda

10 Minutes	Brief discussion of prework (and homework if you are doing these in a series; see chapter 4). Pass out the handout.
15 Minutes	Presentation of the conceptual model or topic
10 Minutes	Initial discussion of the concept using provo/evo questions
15 Minutes	Exercise/application
10 Minutes	Final discussion and assignment of homework

Provo/Evo Discussion Questions

1. Do you know your reputation in the organization?

2. Name some indicators to the type of reputation you have developed.

3. Without naming names, can you think of someone you know from your current job or from past jobs who you think had a poor reputation? How did he or she develop a poor reputation?

4. How should a person go about repairing his or her reputation?

Conceptual Model

Many managers suffer from a poor or inaccurate definition of how their own managers view their performance—their reputation. Unfortunately, this is a common problem and one that gets in the way of a manager's ability to be successful. When you are unaware or unclear about current performance levels, it is more difficult for you to set appropriate goals and targets. Efforts for improvement need to begin with a benchmark, and they should include a plan for transitioning from today's reality to tomorrow's goal. Managers can significantly improve their results when they understand

✓ How their managers would evaluate their performance

✓ The reputation they have in their organization

✓ How well their teams are meeting goals and producing results

✓ How the organization perceives their teams' contributions and effectiveness

✓ Whether or not they are considered good or easy to work with.

It is critical that you know how your superiors, peers, and employees view your performance and managerial style. By establishing the right benchmark, or starting point, improvement plans will be more realistic and operational. The most successful managers have a strong self-awareness. They know how to keep their ears to the ground to listen for valuable information about how they and their teams are doing. The journey from good to great, or great to even greater, is paved with well-planned initiatives and improvement efforts. Managers must understand the reputation they have in their organization, be it positive or disappointing. Peers, managers, and team members respond differently to each manager, based on past results of their work and interactions and how that manager has reacted in good times and bad. The quality of relationships between the manager and others plays a big part in determining a manager's reputation. Managers with poor reputations will find it harder

POWER HOUR #3

to garner support for initiatives and will probably not receive full and helpful collaborative efforts from others. When people say that a manager has a good reputation, they are saying that he or she

- ❖ Can be trusted—Managers are perceived as trustworthy when their words and actions are consistent.

- ❖ Does what he or she promises—Keeping promises means doing what was agreed to, whether the agreement was spoken, written, or implied.

- ❖ Produces good results—Managers who pull their weight and add value to the company are respected and appreciated.

- ❖ Is pleasant or easy to work with—Managers who other staff members like to work with will be perceived more favorably.

- ❖ Is knowledgeable and creative in their chosen field—Manager and peers acknowledge and appreciate middle managers who know their stuff.

- ❖ Is an asset to the company.

When managers have a bad reputation, people may think that they

- ❖ Can't be trusted—Perhaps they have abused confidences or "burned" someone in the past.

- ❖ Don't follow through on commitments—Have they let people down?

- ❖ Don't get the job done when others do—Are their results disappointing?

- ❖ Are in some way difficult to work with—Are they not a team player?

- ❖ Do not have the right skills or aptitude—Do they lack creativity or technical expertise?

❖ Are not an important contributor—Do they make a difference?

Managers can use one or more of the following three approaches to learn their reputation. The first and easiest approach is *to ask*. This method will work in environments where honest and open feedback is available. Managers should also try the second approach—*to observe*—particularly if the first approach does not yield full or truthful information. Many peers, managers, and team members will not feel comfortable being candid with their thoughts. If the first two approaches fail to provide you with the necessary information, then try the third approach, which is *to use an objective third party*. Managers who need to do this will often have a reputation that causes people to be reluctant to provide feedback. Managers should be aware that it is going to be harder to get useful and helpful input as they progress up the ladder in their organization. This is unfortunate, because everyone needs good feedback to perform his or her best.

POWER HOUR #3

Exercise

Self-assess your reputation using the form on the handout (allow 10 minutes). Be prepared to share one area in which you think you would score very well and one area in which you might score lower.

Homework/Application Assignment

Ask your manager and two or three peers to complete the reputation survey. Encourage them to be candid and to remember that your strengths and weaknesses are known—your reputation already exists—and that knowledge gives you power to make changes.

POWER HOUR 3 Handout ❖ Managing and Improving Your Reputation

Management Survey for_____

Please answer the survey openly and honestly. I am interested in learning the good, the bad, and the ugly. I consider this tool to be a part of my overall development plan and value your feedback. Thank you!

Part 1: Management Qualities and Traits

For each trait listed below, indicate whether it is a strength of this manager, a weakness, or somewhere in the middle. If the trait is a weakness, please do not hesitate to point this out. Please also rank these traits from one to seven, with one being the trait this manager is strongest in and seven the trait that is the greatest weakness for him or her.

Management Quality/Trait	Strength	Average	Weakness	Rank
Completes work on time				
Is reliable				
Is easy to work with, even when times are difficult				
Acts quickly and follows up				
Is results oriented				
Is a skilled manager				
Builds and maintains relationships				

Part 2: Open-Ended Questions

Complete the following questions, providing as many specifics as possible:

1. Share a time when this manager let someone down at work.

_____

2. Share the most important contribution this manager has made to the business in the last year.

_____

3. What has been his or her greatest failure in the last year?

_____

(continued)

POWER HOUR 3 Handout ❖ Managing and Improving Your Reputation

4. How well do you believe this manager represents you and your interests?

_____

5. Do you consider this manager highly productive, satisfactorily productive, or below average in productivity?

_____

6. What do people like most and least about working with this manager?
   Most:

_____

   Least:

_____

Part 3: Descriptive Phrases

Each of the following sections contains four phrases. Spread 100 points across the four phrases, giving more points to those phrases that are more descriptive of this manager and his or her performance and fewer points to those phrases that are less descriptive. You can, for example, give 50 points for the first two phrases and 0 points for the other two, or give 30 points for one while giving the others 20, 10, and 40 points, respectively.

This manager's style	*100 Points Total*
Is teamwork oriented	
Values individual initiative and creativity	
Values security and predictability	
Is hard-driving, competitive, and focused on results	
This manager is thought to be	*100 Points Total*
Trustworthy	
Reliable	
A good partner	
Responsible	
When times get tough or busy, this manager	*100 Points Total*
Plans well and is organized	
Can get emotional	
Represents well the needs of his or her team members	
Can get overwhelmed	

POWER HOUR #3 *(side tab)*

POWER HOUR 3 Handout ❖ Managing and Improving Your Reputation

When people say that a manager has a good reputation, they are saying that he or she

- ❖ Can be trusted—Managers are trustworthy when their words and actions are consistent.
- ❖ Does what he or she promises—Keeping promises means doing what was agreed to, whether the agreement was spoken, written, or implied.
- ❖ Produces good results—Managers who pull add value to the company are respected.
- ❖ Is easy to work with—People enjoy working with likable managers.
- ❖ Is knowledgeable and creative in his or her chosen field—Managers and peers acknowledge and appreciate middle managers who know their stuff.
- ❖ Is an asset to the company.

When a manager has a bad reputation, people think that he or she

- ❖ Cannot be trusted—Has he or she "burned" someone in the past?
- ❖ Does not follow through on commitments—Has this manager let people down?
- ❖ Does not get the job done when others do—Are his or her results disappointing?
- ❖ Is in some way difficult to work with—Is this manager not a team player?
- ❖ Does not have the right skills—Does he or she lack creativity or technical expertise?
- ❖ Is not an important contributor—Does he or she make a difference?

POWER HOUR 4:
Your Management A-B Boxes

Prework Assignment

Find a brief, current article or blog post to share with people as a warm-up to this Power Hour. It's OK, and preferred, if the piece is provocative or controversial. The prework should stir conversation and prime people for an exploration of the topic.

Learning Objectives

While completing this Power Hour and the application homework, participants will

1. Discuss the importance of changing management practices to address organizational needs and goals

2. Identify several managerial practices that best support their goals

3. Create a plan to align their daily practices and habits.

Trainer's Objective

Produce a one-hour training session that catalyzes great conversations between managers about management.

Agenda

10 Minutes	Brief discussion of prework (and homework if you are doing these in a series; see chapter 4). Pass out the handout.
15 Minutes	Presentation of the conceptual model or topic
10 Minutes	Initial discussion of the concept using provo/evo questions
15 Minutes	Exercise/application
10 Minutes	Final discussion and assignment of homework.

Provo/Evo Discussion Questions

1. What does it look like when someone tries to solve today's problems using the practices that caused the problem in the first place?

2. Can we create a different result using today's management practices?

3. What types of practices get in our way when trying to improve results?

4. How often should we adjust how we manage?

POWER HOUR #4

Conceptual Model

As our business initiatives and goals change, so too should our leadership and management practices, styles, and approaches. The needs of the business change and so should our leadership. You've heard the saying, "You can't keep doing the same things and get a different result," right? Well, Figure 10.1 takes that simple concept and transforms it into a powerful management tool. Aligning how we lead and manage is critical to short-term and long-term success.

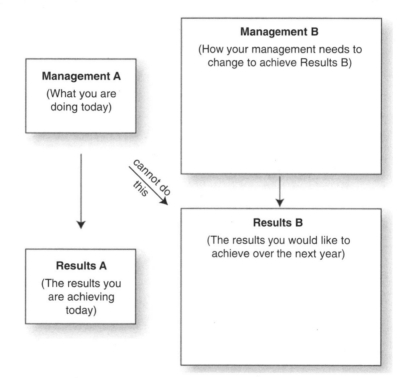

FIGURE 10.1 ❖ Your Management A and B boxes.

Exercise

Ask participants to fill in their B Boxes beginning with Results B then moving up to Management B. Results B should contain the key results they want to achieve over the next year, including how they want to improve their department's results and develop their teams. After 10 minutes, ask people, in pairs, to share their B boxes.

POWER HOUR #4

Homework/Application Assignment

Define what Management B looks like on a daily basis. Create a list of daily habits and regimens that would best personify Management B and support Results B.

POWER HOUR 4 Handout ❖ Your Management A-B Boxes

As our business initiatives and goals change, so should our leadership and management practices, styles, and approaches. Business needs change; so should our leadership. You've heard the saying "You can't keep doing the same things and get a different result. This diagram puts that simple concept into a powerful management tool. Aligning how we lead and manage is critical to short-term and long-term success.

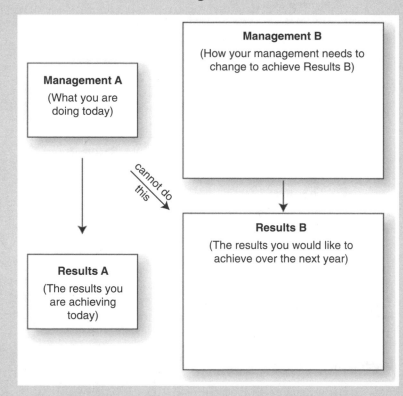

Management A
(What you are doing today)

Management B
(How your management needs to change to achieve Results B)

cannot do this

Results A
(The results you are achieving today)

Results B
(The results you would like to achieve over the next year)

Daily Habits and Practices That Support My Management B Box

_____

_____

CHAPTER 11

POWER HOUR 5: Your Management Filter

Prework Assignment

Find a brief, current article or blog post to share with people as a warm-up to this Power Hour. It's OK, and preferred, if the piece is provocative or controversial. The prework should stir conversation and prime people for an exploration of the topic.

Learning Objectives

While completing this Power Hour and the application homework, participants will

1. Discuss the value of using a decision filter to align decisions with intentions

2. Create a decision filter that aligns with their key goals

3. Begin to use their management filter on a daily basis.

Trainer's Objective

Produce a one-hour training session that catalyzes great conversations between managers about management.

Agenda

10 Minutes	Brief discussion of prework (and homework if you are doing these in a series; see chapter 4). Pass out the handout.
15 Minutes	Presentation of the conceptual model or topic
10 Minutes	Initial discussion of the concept using provo/evo questions
15 Minutes	Exercise/application
10 Minutes	Final discussion and assignment of homework

Provo/Evo Discussion Questions

1. Do leaders sometimes say one thing and do another? Is this intentional?

2. How do you know that your actions and decisions are in alignment with your intentions and goals?

3. Is it realistic to expect that goals and priorities do not conflict with one another?

4. Do you sometimes wish that people would just take a moment to think about the impact of a decision before they make it? Might your employees think this about you?

Conceptual Model

Goals and expectations should form the foundation for how you manage. They create the filters through which you make choices about how to spend your precious time. Once you agree to a set of expectations, they become your general managerial goals—or the ways in which you will manage and the results you have agreed to produce. If you are expected to build a strong and collaborative team environment, this expectation should affect how you plan and facilitate team meetings, how assignments are divvied up, how projects are managed, and how success is measured. You might even change the physical structure of how the office is laid out and the communication tools you use to connect remote team members. If you are charged with building a strong and collaborative team, you will want to ensure that the team environment reinforces collaboration and connection, that team members are trained to collaborate, and that you build a culture of trust and openness. The management practices that build a strong and collaborative team look wildly different than the practices that build a highly individualized and compliant team.

The Management Filter helps managers understand expectations in a way that is concrete and actionable. Creating a Management Filter that supports your general managerial goals—the expectations you have agreed to own—is easy. Think about how each expectation shows up in various aspects of your work. Continuing with the example of building strong and collaborative teams, your filter should prompt you to think about your actions and decisions relative to this expectation. Each day and each week, you can use the filter to make better choices about how you use your time. For example, facilitating collaborative planning sessions or idea-generation meetings should rank pretty high in importance for you. It is also important to align measures and rewards to reinforce collaboration and strong relationships. You need to ask yourself what you can do today that will improve team strength and collaboration. This is a broad goal, but the filter helps you consider the many ways you can have an impact:

❖ Work environment—how working here looks and feels

❖ How meetings are scheduled, planned, and facilitated

❖ How you make and communicate decisions

❖ How roles are structured

❖ Communication and problem-identification processes

❖ How changes are decided, announced, and implemented

❖ How projects are planned, structured, and implemented

❖ How individuals and teams are measured and reinforced

❖ How roles interrelate

❖ How diversity and disagreement is handled

❖ The tasks on which you focus

❖ How you define, communicate, and manage to the expectations you have for your staff and peers

❖ How systems are structured

The Management Filter is a great tool for managers who want to operationalize general managerial goals and expectations. The filter can also help management teams collectively ensure that their actions and decisions are aligned with their common managerial goals for their organizations.

Expectation	Filter Questions: To what degree does taking this action or making this decision...	Level of Support for This Expectation		
Build collaborative teams	encourage and reinforce collaboration and partnership?	LOW	MEDIUM	HIGH
Get projects when promised	enable me and my department to stay on task with our deadlines?	LOW	MEDIUM	HIGH
Demonstrate trust and care	demonstrate my trust in and care for my employees?	LOW	MEDIUM	HIGH
Role model	present a positive and professional image about which I and the company can be proud?	LOW	MEDIUM	HIGH

Exercise

Ask participants to take five minutes to fill out several lines of their Management Filter. Then ask them to share their entries in a small group.

Homework/Application Assignment

Complete your Management Filter and update it often. Take it to meetings and consider it when making decisions or choosing priorities.

POWER HOUR 5 Handout ❖ Your Management Filter

Goals and expectations should form the foundation for how you manage—they create the filters from which you make choices about how to spend your precious time. Once you agree to a set of expectations, they become your general managerial goals. If you are expected to build a strong and collaborative team environment, this expectation should affect how you plan and facilitate team meetings, how assignments are divvied up, how projects are managed, and how success is measured. You might even change the physical structure of how the office is laid out and the communication tools you use to connect remote team members. The Management Filter helps managers understand expectations in a way that is concrete and actionable. Creating a Management Filter that supports your general managerial goals—the expectations you have agreed to own—is easy. Think about how each expectation shows up in various aspects of your work.

The filter helps you consider several possible ways that you can have an impact:

❖ Work environment—how working here looks and feels

❖ How meetings are scheduled, planned, and facilitated

❖ How you make and communicate decisions

❖ How roles are structured

❖ Communication and problem-identification processes

❖ How changes are decided, announced, and implemented

(continued)

POWER HOUR #5

POWER HOUR 5 Handout ❖ Your Management Filter

- ❖ How projects are planned, structured, and implemented
- ❖ How individuals and teams are measured and reinforced
- ❖ How roles interrelate
- ❖ How diversity and disagreement are handled
- ❖ The tasks on which you focus
- ❖ How you define, communicate, and manage to the expectations you have for your staff and peers
- ❖ How systems are structured

The Management Filter is a great tool for managers who want to operationalize general managerial goals—expectations. Use the following charts to evaluate your own expectations. Some samples are given, but space is provided so you can write in your own observations.

Expectation	Filter Questions: To what degree does taking this action or making this decision...	Level of Support for This Expectation		
Build collaborative teams	encourage and reinforce collaboration and partnership?	LOW	MEDIUM	HIGH
Get projects when promised	enable me and my department to stay on task with our deadlines?	LOW	MEDIUM	HIGH
Demonstrate trust and care	demonstrate my trust in and care for my employees?	LOW	MEDIUM	HIGH
Role model	present a positive and professional image about which I can be proud?	LOW	MEDIUM	HIGH

(continued)

POWER HOUR #5

90

POWER HOUR 5 Handout ❖ Your Management Filter

Expectation	Filter Questions: To what degree does taking this action or making this decision...	Level of Support for This Expectation		
		LOW	MEDIUM	HIGH
		LOW	MEDIUM	HIGH
		LOW	MEDIUM	HIGH
		LOW	MEDIUM	HIGH
		LOW	MEDIUM	HIGH
		LOW	MEDIUM	HIGH
		LOW	MEDIUM	HIGH
		LOW	MEDIUM	HIGH
		LOW	MEDIUM	HIGH
		LOW	MEDIUM	HIGH
		LOW	MEDIUM	HIGH
		LOW	MEDIUM	HIGH
		LOW	MEDIUM	HIGH

POWER HOUR #5

CHAPTER 12

POWER HOUR 6: Mind Your Metrics!

Prework Assignment

Find a brief, current article or blog post to share with people as a warm-up to this Power Hour. It's OK, and preferred, if the piece is provocative or controversial. The prework should stir conversation and prime people for an exploration of the topic.

Learning Objectives

While completing this Power Hour and the application homework, participants will

1. Discuss the importance of correctly measuring success

2. Identify key metrics that indicate how well their departments are performing

3. Create a plan to measure and communicate the top three indicators of departmental success and health.

Trainer's Objective

The trainer's objective is to produce a one-hour training session that catalyzes great conversations between managers about management.

Agenda

10 Minutes	Brief discussion of prework (and homework if you are doing these in a series; see chapter 4). Pass out the handout.
15 Minutes	Presentation of the conceptual model or topic
10 Minutes	Initial discussion of the concept using provo/evo questions
15 Minutes	Exercise/application
10 Minutes	Final discussion and assignment of homework

Provo/Evo Discussion Questions

1. Do you know how well or poorly your team and department are performing?

2. If things are going well, how do you know they are going well? If things are going poorly, how will you know why?

3. Look at the measures you have in place today. Do they focus on what matters most?

4. Is it more important to know why things fail or why they succeed? Do we measure one more than the other?

5. Do you measure too many things or not enough of them?

Conceptual Model

Good information allows you to make better decisions. Better decisions lead to improved results. Do you know how well your team is performing? What measures do you look at on a daily, weekly, or monthly basis? If you look at the right data, you can make good decisions and ensure your success. If your metrics don't tell the whole story or the accurate story of what's going on in your business, you could be headed for failure and not know it. Managers should know what's going on in their departments.

Measures can offer early warning signs that a project is getting off track or that barriers are getting in the way of results. Picking the right measures takes a bit of work, but don't let metrics and analysis intimidate you. Once you adopt a regular routine for looking at the business from an analytical perspective, you will feel much more comfortable working with the data.

When selecting measures, think about what excellence looks like to your internal and external customers. Take some time to create the right measures (but just a few) that will tell you what you need to know about your part of the business. Determine the right metrics for your area, then create a practice for how those metrics are measured, updated, and communicated. Be as transparent as possible. Information is power, and the more your team members are aware of what's working and what's not, the better they will be able to be a proactive part of the team's success.

Metrics allow you and your team to discuss your part of the business with some accuracy and specificity. Your conversations will be richer and make a greater difference when enhanced by the knowledge of good metrics. When you create measurement practices, you are putting the metrics into your daily and weekly regimens. You are inviting the data into the department as a respected partner. Here are a few examples of ways to create measurement practices:

✓ Involve the entire team in selecting and measuring metrics.

✓ Measure results regularly so that it becomes habit.

✓ Talk about metrics at team meetings. Don't just review them; engage in meaty conversation about what the metrics are telling you and your team members.

✓ Post metrics on common walls, on the intranet, and on your office walls.

✓ Acknowledge and celebrate successes.

POWER HOUR #6

If you and your team are crystal clear about the results you need to achieve, collect crisp metrics that tell you how you are doing, and, if you regularly discuss these metrics, your results will improve. We achieve what we pay attention to.

Exercise

Ask participants to answer the following two questions (in five minutes) and then go around the room and ask each person to share his or her answer (for 10 minutes).

1. What's the most important contribution that you and your team can make to the business?

2. How can you measure the performance of this contribution?

Homework/Application Assignment

Use the "Determining Metrics" worksheet to involve your team in making sure you are measuring what's most important. Select three metrics to track and communicate with your team about on a regular basis.

POWER HOUR 6 Handout ❖ Mind Your Metrics!

Good information allows you to make better decisions. Better decisions lead to improved results. Do you know how well your team is performing? What measures do you look at on a daily, weekly, or monthly basis? If you look at the right data, you can make good decisions and ensure your success. If your metrics don't tell the whole story or the accurate story of what's going on in your business, you could be headed for failure and not know it. Managers should know what's going on in their departments. Measures can offer early warning signs that a project is getting off track or that barriers are getting in the way of results. Picking

(continued)

POWER HOUR #6

POWER HOUR 6 Handout ❖ Mind Your Metrics!

the right measures takes a bit of work, but don't let metrics and analysis intimidate you. Once you adopt a regular routine for looking at the business from an analytical perspective, you will feel much more comfortable working with the data.

When selecting measures, think about what excellence looks like to your internal and external customers. Take some time to create the right measures (but just a few) that will tell you what you need to know about your part of the business. Determine the right metrics for your area, then create a practice for how those metrics are measured, updated, and communicated. Be as transparent as possible. Information is power, and the more your team members are aware of what's working and what's not, the better they will be able to be a proactive part of the team's success.

Metrics allow you and your team to discuss your part of the business with some accuracy and specificity. Your conversations will be richer and make a greater difference when enhanced by the knowledge of good metrics. When you create measurement practices, you are putting the metrics into your daily and weekly regimens. You are inviting the data into the department as a respected partner. Here are a few examples of ways to create measurement practices:

✓ Involve the entire team in selecting and measuring metrics.

✓ Measure results regularly (the same time every month), so that it becomes habit.

✓ Talk about metrics at team meetings. Don't just review them; engage in meaty conversation about what the metrics are telling you and your team members.

✓ Post metrics on common walls, on the intranet, and on your office walls.

✓ Acknowledge and celebrate successes.

If you and your team are crystal clear about the results you need to achieve, collect crisp metrics that tell you how you are doing, and, if you regularly discuss these metrics, your results will improve. We achieve what we pay attention to. The following questions should help.

(continued)

POWER HOUR #6

POWER HOUR 6 Handout ❖ Mind Your Metrics!

1. What's the most important contribution that you and your team can make to the business?

_____

_____

2. How can you measure the performance of this contribution?

_____

_____

Determining Metrics Worksheet

1. Why does this team exist? In what ways is it expected to contribute to the company?

_____

_____

_____

2. What are your current department metrics, and what is your current level of performance on these metrics?

_____

_____

_____

3. Do these measures indicate how well your department is performing against the key areas in which the company requests your team to contribute?

_____

_____

_____

(continued)

POWER
HOUR #6

Determining Metrics Worksheet

4. If you were to ask your key internal or external customers, would they think these metrics are most important? If not, what indicators would your customers advocate that you measure?

_____

_____

_____

5. Can you score well on these metrics and produce poor results? If so, why?

_____

_____

_____

6. If you could look at only two indicators of the team's results, what would those two indicators be? What's the best way to measure these indicators? At what frequency should you measure and review these indicators? Who should own collecting and communicating the data? How are we performing against these metrics today—do we know? (If not, determine that very quickly and have another quick review meeting with the team.)

_____

_____

_____

_____

_____

7. How should we move forward?

_____

_____

_____

POWER HOUR #6

CHAPTER 13

POWER HOUR 7: Grand Slam Home Runs

Prework Assignment

Find a brief, current article or blog post to share with people as a warm-up to this Power Hour. It's OK, and preferred, if the piece is provocative or controversial. The prework should stir conversation and prime people for an exploration of the topic.

Learning Objectives

While completing this Power Hour and the application homework, participants will

1. Define *grand slam home runs* in business

2. Create one grand slam home run goal

3. Communicate the grand slam home run goal with team members

4. Implement actions in support of success in achieving goals.

Trainer's Objective

The trainer's objective is to produce a one-hour training session that catalyzes great conversations between managers about management.

Agenda

10 Minutes	Brief discussion of prework (and homework if you are doing these in a series; see chapter 4). Pass out the handout.
15 Minutes	Presentation of the conceptual model or topic
10 Minutes	Initial discussion of the concept using provo/evo questions
15 Minutes	Exercise/application
10 Minutes	Final discussion and assignment of homework

Provo/Evo Discussion Questions

1. When is good, good enough?

2. Do you know what your manager would consider to be a grand slam home run goal?

3. When was the last time you or your team achieved a grand slam home run? What made it a grand slam?

4. If you define and agree to grand slam home run goals, are you shooting yourself in the foot?

Conceptual Model

There are days that make you feel daily challenges are demanding 100 percent of your attention, but managers are *not* just cogs in the corporate wheel. They're the engines, and they set the pace of the work, workplace, and results. The last thing you want to do is sit back and let daily to-dos flood your brain and body from morning until evening, right? There are far too many good things to do in any given day. You and your team need to focus on the few great things that will move work forward. You want to feel like a success, and you want your team to win and thrive. You want to produce outstanding work—products and services—that make you proud. Anyone can produce results, but only the best managers can produce results that make a big difference.

Grand slam home run is a term from baseball. When a batter hits the ball out of the park (and not into foul territory), this is called a home run. The batter then gets to run the bases and collect a run, or one point. If there are any players already on a base (first, second, or third base), they get to run to home plate, too, and collect a run. When a batter hits a home run and the bases are loaded (all three bases have runners), this is called a grand slam home run because it results in the highest possible number of points—four runs or four points. The grand slam makes the most out of the team's efforts and has an added benefit of creating a feeling of success throughout the organization.

The grand slam is a great benchmark for managerial results because everything you do should have a positive and additive effect on your team, peers, and the organization. If you are going to do something, make it a grand slam!

Ask your manager to clarify the results you and your team need to produce over the next year. For each key result, ask him or her what a grand slam would look like. For example, if a key result is to successfully implement the new accounting system within budget by August 1, a grand slam home run might be to

❖ Complete the implementation by July 1, before the busy season

❖ Involve the accounting team in the project, such that ownership and acceptance is high

❖ Implement the project while improving accountant computer skills (so they can better use the new system's features)

❖ Develop robust contingency plans to cover any potential project setbacks

❖ Find a way to do all this and reduce the costs spent on the project—to harness the creativity of the group to find the best way to transition to the new system.

There's getting a project done and then there's doing a project such that many other aspects of the work are improved as well. That's great planning and management. As a driven and talented manager, you want to know what excellence looks like. Actually, you need to know because you need to be able to define excellence for your team. Define and strive for the grand slam home run to have the deepest and broadest positive impact on the organization.

Exercise

Ask participants to select one major goal that their teams are working on (or are about to work on) and redefine it in terms of what a grand slam home run would look like (10 minutes). Ask participants to share their grand slam home run goals in pairs.

Homework/Application Assignment

Share your grand slam home run goal with your manager and team members and get their input. Align your thinking and actions to go for the grand slam!

POWER HOUR 7 Handout ❖ Grand Slam Home Runs

Some days make you feel like the daily fires are demanding 100 percent of your attention, but managers are *not* just cogs in the corporate wheel. They're the engines, and they set the pace of the work, workplace, and results. The last thing you want to do is sit back and let the fire hose of

(continued)

POWER HOUR 7 Handout ❖ **Grand Slam Home Runs**

daily to-dos flood your brain and body from morning until evening, right? There are far too many good things to do in any given day. You and your team need to focus on the few great things that will move work forward. You want to feel like a success, and you want your teams to win and thrive. You want to produce outstanding work—products and services—that make you proud. Anyone can produce results, but only the best managers can produce results that make a big difference.

The grand slam home run is a great benchmark for managerial results because everything you do should have a positive and additive affect on your teams, peers, and the organization. If you are going to do something, make it a grand slam!

Ask your manager to clarify the results you and your team need to produce over the next year. For each key result, ask him or her what a grand slam home run would look like. For example, if a key result is to successfully implement the new accounting system within budget by August 1, a grand slam home run might be to

❖ Complete the implementation by July 1, before the busy season

❖ Involve the accounting team in the project, such that ownership and acceptance is high

❖ Implement the project while improving accountant computer skills (so they can better use the new system's features)

❖ Develop robust contingency plans to cover any potential setbacks

❖ Find a way to do all this and reduce the costs spent on the project—to harness the creativity of the group to find the best way to transition to the new system.

There's getting a project done, and then there's doing a project such that many other aspects of the work are improved as well. That's great planning and management. As a driven and talented manager, you want to know what excellence looks like. Actually, you need to know because you need to be able to define excellence for your team. Use the following sections to define your goal and strive for the grand slam home run, to have the deepest and broadest positive impact on the organization.

(continued)

POWER HOUR #7

My Grand Slam Home Run Goal

_____

_____

_____

_____

Goal	What a Grand Slam Home Run Looks Like	Why This Is a Grand Slam
Implement new booking engine by end of second quarter within budget.	Booking engine is implemented and welcomed by the staff. You have created contingency plans and ensured everyone is trained and feels comfortable with the new system before the switch is flipped. You have used this opportunity to train back-up staff. You have created a positive momentum and excitement for the change that will fuel and support the next phases of booking development.	You are making a major change while reducing risk and increasing people's comfort and competence with the new system. You are taking the time and initiative to get people involved and active with the new system. You are building the team's energy for and ability to transition.
Cross-train staff by end of year without going over budget.	Use the cross training as a way to better get to know people's strengths and career goals. Create a cross-training plan that builds collaboration and coopera-tion among people	The plan is robust and more likely to be implemented as planned. Most cross-training plans get set aside because they don't account for

(continued)

POWER HOUR 7 Handout ❖ **Grand Slam Home Runs Goal**

Goal	What a Grand Slam Home Run Looks Like	Why This Is a Grand Slam
	in different jobs. Build a plan that can account for absences and vacations so that the cross training does not get set aside if someone is out sick. Cross-train at least two people for each position.	changes. The plan also reinforces your need to create better relationships and understand people's strengths and career interests.
Develop and implement a product development review process by July 31	Take the time to talk to key stakeholders before creating the process. Create a process that will be widely supported by key stakeholders and that respects everyone's precious time. The process should include practices that will allow the review to continue in the event that some participants are out of town. The process ought to be inclusive, but the number of people sitting in meetings should not get out of hand. Create a process that will ensure that product managers collect and communicate key analysis and metrics before the review meetings occur.	Creating the project with these considerations will ensure that people are prepared to participate and decisions can be made in a timely manner. This approach will also support your goal both to use time wisely and to be inclusive.

POWER HOUR #7

CHAPTER 14

POWER HOUR 8:
Defining Excellence

Prework Assignment

Find a brief, current article or blog post to share with people as a warm-up to this Power Hour. It's OK, and preferred, if the piece is provocative or controversial. The prework should stir conversation and prime people for an exploration of the topic.

Learning Objectives

While completing this Power Hour and the application homework, participants will

1. Discuss the importance of defining excellence

2. Define what excellence looks like for their teams

3. Communicate their view of excellence to their teams within a week of the training.

Trainer's Objective

The trainer's objective is to produce a one-hour training session that catalyzes great conversations between managers about management.

Agenda

10 Minutes	Brief discussion of prework (and homework if you are doing these in a series; see chapter 4). Pass out the handout.
15 Minutes	Presentation of the conceptual model or topic
10 Minutes	Initial discussion of the concept using provo/evo questions
15 Minutes	Exercise/application
10 Minutes	Final discussion and assignment of homework

Provo/Evo Discussion Questions

1. Do your employees know how you define excellence?

2. How might they know what excellent performance looks like?

3. In absence of you telling them, how might employees surmise what excellence is?

4. Do you think that your employees would do things differently if they had a crystal clear view of how you measure excellence?

Conceptual Model

It's too bad that we don't talk more about excellence. Excellent performance, after all, is very, very good! A common reason why we don't see more excellent performance is because we don't talk about what excellence really looks like and how we would know it if we saw it in action. Talking about excellence is powerful. Conversations create reality. Spend time talking about excellence, and it is likely that you will get more excellent performance. People make individual choices about what to do and how to do it based on their understanding of expectations and their individual motivation. Managers want to make sure that the filter individuals are using is a good one.

In order to talk more about excellence, you need to define excellence and describe it in ways that bring it to life. Saying that excellence means doing a great job is a cop-out and not helpful. Imagine that your team members are thriving and performing at the top of their game. Now look around this imaginary place and write down what you see. How are people communicating? How do people spend their time? What happens when problems arise? In what ways are team members showing creativity and what kind of innovation do you see happening? Describe what it looks like when projects exceed expectations. What does learning and relationship building look like?

Create a one-page description of excellence for your department, then an additional paragraph or two for each unique position. It's fine to involve your team in creating a vision of excellence, but first your team members need to know how you define excellence. Here is an example for a management team:

Managerial Excellence at _____ :

POWER HOUR #8

- ✓ You and your team are focused on what's most important, and you produce excellent results. People work at a brisk pace, but they do not feel burned out. Employees are clear about priorities and how their work ties to departmental and corporate goals.

- ✓ Your work environment encourages team members to do their best work and execute it well. They feel challenged and important. Communication is open, candid, and focused on the business. Although they know they are

111

accountable for results, employees are driven by their intrinsic motivation to excel and accomplish.

✓ You know time is a precious resource, and you ensure that both you and your team use it wisely. Meetings are called only when necessary, and they are well run. Conversations are lively, provocative, evocative, and focused. People are eager to participate in business dialogue and contribute their ideas and concerns. You and your team have become master conversationalists. Even so, you do not bog people down with unnecessary meetings, emails, conference calls, or written material.

✓ You know that saying "No" is just as important as saying, "Yes." You demonstrate focus and courage to make sure that your team does not get buried with projects or tasks that are nice to do but would not make it to the list of what's most important. You productively partner with your manager and peers to collectively choose the work that will best support the company's goals, and you reject projects that do not. Your focus helps you and your team produce results and serve your internal and external customers.

✓ You have tuned your department to best serve the needs of your internal and external customers. You aggressively eliminate barriers to providing outstanding service and reengineer processes and practices that support your operations. You acknowledge the importance of serving internal customers such that external customers are better served and satisfied. You proactively work with peers to ensure that interdepartmental processes and practices are effective.

✓ The only constant is change. You and your team are able to nimbly respond to changing needs and conditions. You respond to emerging needs and do not hesitate to readjust tasks and workflow when needed. You help your team adjust and deal with change.

✓ You know you are the face of your company, and you play an important role in helping it grow and mature. You role-model excellence and are a pleasure to work with. You are regarded as trustworthy and reliable. Employees want to be a member of your team, and they know you will support their needs and goals. You take administrative responsibilities seriously and complete forms and reports on time. As an agent for the company, you make good judgments on its behalf and protect it from unacceptable risk.

This is what managerial excellence looks like and we know that each of our managers is capable of achieving this level of contribution. Some of you might need to question a few habits or learn new skills. The journey will be well worth it. Imagine what work will feel like when you reach managerial excellence. The impact you will have on the organization will be inspiring and significant, and will have tangible results. You will feel like you make a difference every day. Strong teams will stay together and do great work. Your company will be a better, stronger, and more sought-after organization—both by customers and by prospective employees.

Exercise

Break the group into subgroups of three or four, then assign each subgroup one of the following question to answer:

1. What does excellence look like in meetings?

2. What does excellence look like on project teams?

3. What does excellence look like with regard to time management?

4. What does excellence look like with regard to productivity?

After five minutes, ask each group to share their responses.

Homework/Application Assignment

Come up with your own definition of excellence and communicate it to your team in the coming week.

POWER HOUR #8

POWER HOUR 8 Handout ❖ Defining Excellence

A common reason why we don't see more excellent performance is because we don't talk about what excellence really looks like and how we would know it if we saw it in action. Talking about excellence is powerful. Conversations create reality. Spend time talking about excellence, and it is likely that you will encounter excellent performance more often.

In order to talk more about excellence, you need to define it and describe it in ways that bring it to life. Saying excellence is doing a great job is a cop out and unhelpful.

Develop a one-page description of excellence for your department. Include an additional paragraph or two for each unique position. It's fine to involve your team members in creating a vision of excellence, but they need to know how you define it.

Imagine that your team members are thriving and performing at the top of their game. Now look around this imaginary place and write down what you see. How are people communicating? How do people spend their time? What happens when problems arise? In what ways are team members showing creativity, and what kind of innovation do you see happening? Describe what it looks like when projects exceed expectations. What does learning and relationship-building look like?

Contextual Element	How You Define Excellence for This Element
Communication	
Collaboration	
Professionalism	
Creativity and Innovation	
Project Performance	
Meetings	
Problem Identification and Solving	
Change and Agility	
Results and Performance	
The Team and Organization	

(continued)

POWER HOUR 8 Handout ❖ **Defining Excellence**

Example (for a Management Team):

You and your team are focused on what's most important, and you produce excellent results. People work at a brisk pace, but they do not feel burned out. Employees are clear about priorities and how their work ties into departmental and corporate goals.

Your work environment encourages team members to do their best work and execute it well. They feel challenged and important. Communication is open, candid, and focused on the business. Although they know they are accountable for results, employees are driven by their intrinsic motivation to excel and accomplish.

You know time is a precious resource and you ensure that you and your team use it wisely. Meetings are called only when necessary, and they are well run. Conversations are lively, provocative, evocative, and focused. People are eager to participate in business dialogue and contribute their ideas and concerns. You and your team have become master conversationalists. Even so, you do not bog people down with unnecessary meetings, emails, conference calls, or written material.

You know that saying "No" is just as important as saying "Yes." You demonstrate focus and courage to make sure that your team does not get buried by projects or tasks that are nice to do but are not what's most important. You productively partner with your manager and peers to collectively choose the work that will best support the company's goals, and you reject projects that do not. Your focus helps you and your team produce results and serve your internal and external customers.

You have tuned your department to best serve the needs of your internal and external customers. You aggressively eliminate barriers to providing outstanding service and reengineer processes and practices that support your operations. You acknowledge the importance of serving internal customers such that external customers are better served and satisfied. You proactively work with peers to ensure that interdepartmental processes and practices are effective.

The only constant is change. You and your team are able to nimbly respond to changing needs and conditions. You respond to emerging

(continued)

POWER HOUR #8

POWER HOUR 8 Handout ❖ Defining Excellence

needs and do not hesitate to readjust tasks and work flow when needed. You help your team adjust and come to terms with change.

You know you are the face of your company and play an important role in helping it grow and mature. You role model excellence and are a pleasure to work with. You are regarded as trustworthy and reliable. Employees want to be a member of your team and they know you will support their needs and goals. You take administrative responsibilities seriously and complete forms and reports on time. As an agent for the company, you make good judgments on its behalf and protect it from unacceptable risk.

This is what managerial excellence looks like and we know that each of our managers is capable of achieving this level of contribution. Some of you might need to question a few habits or learn new skills. The journey will be well worth it. Imagine what work will feel like when you reach managerial excellence. The impact you will have on the organization will be inspiring and significant in terms of tangible results. You will feel like you make a difference every day. Strong teams will stay together and do great work. Your company will be a better, stronger, and more sought-after organization—both by customers and by prospective employees.

CHAPTER 15

POWER HOUR 9: Communicating Expectations

Prework Assignment

Find a brief, current article or blog post to share with people as a warm-up to this Power Hour. It's OK, and preferred, if the piece is provocative or controversial. The prework should stir conversation and prime people for an exploration of the topic.

Learning Objectives

While completing this Power Hour and the application homework, participants will

1. Discuss the importance of clarifying expectations

2. Learn the recommended elements for clarifying expectations

3. Define and communicate expectations for at least one employee within one month of the training.

Trainer's Objective:

Produce a one-hour training session that catalyzes great conversations between managers about management.

Agenda:

10 Minutes	Brief discussion of prework (and homework if you are doing these in a series; see chapter 4). Pass out the handout.
15 Minutes	Presentation of the conceptual model or topic
10 Minutes	Initial discussion of the concept using provo/evo questions
15 Minutes	Exercise/application
10 Minutes	Final discussion and assignment of homework

Provo/Evo Discussion Questions

1. Do your employees know what you expect of them? How do they know?

2. How often do your expectations change? How do you ensure that people understand the changes?

3. How many times per year should managers and employees discuss expectations? What's practical?

4. If you were to take the time to fully express expectations based on these recommended elements, what would be most likely to surprise your employees?

Conceptual Model

As a manager, you can immediately improve the focus and productivity of your team members by ensuring that they know what is expected of them. When high-impact middle managers talk to their employees, they go beyond discussing obvious expectations. They ensure that each person has a good understanding of how they can best contribute to the company. Notice the significant difference between the list of expectations usually discussed by managers and those that are recommended for discussion. Here are the expectations that are usually discussed:

❖ Required tasks

❖ Work on specific projects

❖ Regular and ongoing work for which the employee is responsible

❖ The types of tasks that this person should own

❖ An expectation to bring questions and problems to the manager.

Here are those that are recommended for discussion:

❖ Expectations about how this person should contribute to identifying and solving problems

❖ Expectations about how this person will represent their function and the company

❖ Expectations about generating new ideas and improving results

❖ Expectations about how this employee should analyze and manage organizational resources (e.g., staff, finances, equipment)

❖ Expectations about how this person will manage employees

❖ Expectations about the business relationships this person should develop and maintain

POWER HOUR #9

119

❖ Expectations about deadlines, execution, and results

❖ Expectations about judgment and decisions

❖ Expectations about meeting preparedness and participation

❖ Expectations about planning and communicating work

❖ Expectations of how this person needs to improve his or her performance.

The list of topics recommended for discussion may seem long, but it is necessary to ensure that each person fully understands what he or she expected to accomplish. Managers who use this method of setting expectations will notice an immediate and welcome difference in their employee's focus because this approach fully communicates the breadth and importance of each person's role. Some employees may find this approach daunting initially; however, the ones who truly want to excel and do quality work will find this clarification of expectations motivating.

Do not to get too prescriptive when discussing expectations. For example, it can be helpful to let employees know how often they should provide progress updates. It is not helpful to define what the planning report should look like, to instruct in how to disseminate work assignments, or to create the list of tasks to be included in the first report. That is micromanagement. Expectation conversations establish the measuring stick for performance, not the blueprint for how the employee is to conduct his or her work. If the employee could use a few tips on how to accomplish a task or project, schedule a separate coaching discussion to address this need.

A successful discussion will set up a powerful foundation for optimal performance and productivity. Clearly communicating expectations accomplishes more than any other performance management activity and is at the top of the 80/20 list of great and right work to do. Before the discussion begins, however, you'll want to prepare:

✓ Think about and write down expectations. Type them up and make a copy to share with the employee.

✓ Talk to peers and other managers to ensure that assumptions about improvement areas are correct.

✓ Schedule the meeting at a time that is conducive to a relaxed and thorough discussion (not 30 minutes before a big meeting, or 4:30 p.m. on Friday).

✓ Let the employee know that this discussion will focus on ensuring that he or she is clear about what is expected and how he or she can make a significant contribution to the company. Explain that clarifying expectations helps managers stay focused and successful. Other staff members will be scheduled for similar conversations.

You'll also need a plan for conducting the discussion:

✓ This is no time to be wimpy or general—share expectations in clear, specific, and resolute terms.

✓ Express expectations in a "matter-of-fact" manner. This is important to reduce the emotional content of the discussion. Expectation conversations should not become a sermon, plea, or sales pitch.

✓ Focus on the essential outcome—but allow some latitude on how to get there.

✓ Never assume that expectations are clear. Cover all expectations.

✓ Answer requests for clarification, but do not allow the meeting to creep into other topics. The desired outcome of this discussion is that expectations are clear and understood.

Finally, plan for after the discussion:

✓ Once the initial discussion has taken place, expectations can be reinforced in a variety of day-to-day settings. Doing so will also help others in the organization understand each person's role and responsibilities.

✓ Be sure to follow up on expectations that are not being met. Do not wait to address concerns or issues, because doing so implies that it was not really an expectation.

POWER HOUR #9

121

Many employees do not fully understand what is expected of them, which is a shame because uncertainty impairs satisfaction, productivity, and results. By clarifying expectations, you can ensure that your employees are focused on the right objectives and set up for success.

Exercise

Ask each person to select one of the bulleted items from the list of recommended discussion items and create a one- or two-sentence expression of their expectations for their team members. Give them five minutes to work, then ask for several volunteers to share their statements.

Homework/Application Assignment

Define expectations for your team and share expectations with at least one employee over the next month.

POWER HOUR 9 Handout ❖ Communicating Expectations

As a manager, you can immediately improve the focus and productivity of your team members by ensuring that they know what is expected of them. When high-impact middle managers talk to their employees, they go beyond discussing obvious expectations. They ensure that each person has a good understanding of how they can best contribute to the company. Notice the significant difference between the expectations discussed by most managers and those that are recommended. The usual conversation about expectations includes several topics:

❖ Required tasks

❖ Work on specific projects

❖ Regular and ongoing work for which the employee is responsible

(continued)

POWER HOUR 9 Handout ❖ **Communicating Expectations**

❖ The types of tasks that this person should own

❖ An expectation to bring questions and problems to the manager.

Here is a list of recommended topics for a conversation about expectations:

❖ Expectations about how this person should contribute to identifying and solving problems

❖ Expectations about how this person will represent their function and the company

❖ Expectations about generating new ideas and improving results

❖ Expectations about how this employee should analyze and manage organizational resources (e.g., staff, finances, equipment)

❖ Expectations about how this person will manage employees

❖ Expectations about the business relationships this person should maintain and develop

❖ Expectations about deadlines, execution, and results

❖ Expectations about judgment and decisions

❖ Expectations about meeting preparedness and participation

❖ Expectations about planning and communicating work

❖ Expectations of how this person needs to improve his or her performance.

The recommended list of discussion topics may seem long, but it is necessary to ensure that each person fully understands what he or she is expected to accomplish. Managers who use this method of setting expectations will notice an immediate and welcome difference in their employee's focus because this approach fully communicates the breadth and importance of each person's role. Some employees may find this daunting initially; however, the ones who truly want to excel and who do quality work will find this clarification of expectations motivating.

(continued)

POWER HOUR #9

POWER HOUR 9 Handout ❖ Communicating Expectations

Do not to get too prescriptive when discussing expectations. For example, it can be helpful to let the employee know how often he or she should provide progress updates. It is not helpful to define what the planning report should look like, to determine how to disseminate work assignments, or to create the list of tasks included in the first report. That is micromanagement. Expectation conversations establish the measuring stick for performance, not the blueprint for how the employee is to conduct his or her work. If the employee could use a few tips on how to accomplish a task or project, schedule a separate coaching discussion to address this need.

A successful discussion will set up a powerful foundation for optimal performance and productivity. Clearly communicating expectations accomplishes more than any other performance management activity and is at the top of the 80/20 list of great and right work to do. Before the discussion, plan your approach:

❖ Think about and write down expectations. Type them up and make a copy to share with the employee.

❖ Talk to peers and other managers to ensure that assumptions about improvement areas are correct.

❖ Schedule the meeting at a time that is conducive to a relaxed and thorough discussion (not 30 minutes before a big meeting, or 4:30 p.m. on a Friday).

❖ Let the employee know that this discussion will focus on ensuring that he or she is clear about what is expected and how he or she can make a significant contribution to the company. Explain that clarifying expectations helps managers stay focused and successful. Other staff members will be scheduled for similar conversations.

You'll also need a plan for during the discussion:

❖ This is no time to be wimpy or general—share expectations in clear, specific, and resolute terms.

(continued)

POWER HOUR 9 Handout: Communicating Expectations

❖ Express expectations in a "matter-of-fact" manner. This is important to reduce the emotional content of the discussion. Expectation conversations should not become a sermon, plea, or sales pitch.

❖ Focus on the essential outcome—but allow some latitude on how to get there.

❖ Never *assume* that expectations are clear. Cover all expectations.

❖ Answer requests for clarification, but do not allow the meeting discussion to creep into other topics. The desired outcome of this discussion is that expectations are clear and understood.

Finally, have a plan for after the discussion:

❖ Once the initial discussion has taken place, expectations can be reinforced in a variety of day-to-day settings. Doing so will also help others in the organization understand each person's role and responsibilities.

❖ Be sure to follow up on expectations that are not being met. Do not wait to address concerns or issues, because doing so implies that it was not really an expectation.

Many employees do not fully understand what is expected of them, which is a shame because uncertainty impairs satisfaction, productivity, and results. By clarifying expectations, you can ensure that your employees are focused on the right objectives and are set up for success.

POWER HOUR #9

CHAPTER 16

POWER HOUR 10: The Art of Planning

Prework Assignment

Find a brief, current article or blog post to share with people as a warm-up to this Power Hour. It's OK, and preferred, if the piece is provocative or controversial. The prework should stir conversation and prime people for an exploration of the topic.

Learning Objectives

While completing this Power Hour and the application homework, participants will

1. Discuss the importance of planning

2. Identify positive daily and weekly planning habits

3. Create and communicate a plan for the coming week.

POWER HOUR #10

127

Trainer's Objective

The trainer's objective is to produce a one-hour training session that catalyzes great conversations between managers about management.

Agenda

10 Minutes	Brief discussion of prework (and homework if you are doing these in a series; see chapter 4). Pass out the handout.
15 Minutes	Presentation of the conceptual model or topic
10 Minutes	Initial discussion of the concept using provo/evo questions
15 Minutes	Exercise/application
10 Minutes	Final discussion and assignment of homework

Provo/Evo Discussion Questions

To further the goal of this Power Hour, consider these questions:

1. Over a given day or week, how much time should you spend planning? How much time do you currently spend?

2. How do you plan? What are your most effective habits or rituals?

3. How would your employees rate your ability to plan?

4. What gets in the way of planning?

Conceptual Model

Planning is critical, yet it is performed relatively rarely. You can be more focused and successful if you spend just a few minutes each day planning. By definition, planning is not something that has to be done right now—it is not urgent—which makes it a perfect target for procrastination. Of course, we all know that choosing to procrastinate will only come back to haunt us later, because if we don't plan, today's urgent tasks are likely to appear unexpectedly.

Planning is the act of thinking about the contribution that you and your team can make today (this week, this month, this year, this decade), then choosing the actions that will best support your intent. Planning is not boring and not mundane—it's where managerial magic happens, because it's where you make the decisions about how to spend your precious time and how to best focus your team's energies, passions, and strengths.

Planning is like going on a shopping spree with $5,000 in cash in your hands: Choosing what to buy is fun, but it is important that you choose wisely! Your time and your team's time is the $5,000. For some of you, the cost of your team's time is much more than $5,000 a day. How will you spend your $5,000? Will you blow it on short-term needs and wants, or will you invest in the future? Effective planning will help both you and your team maximize your impact on today's and tomorrow's results. To improve your planning skills, I recommend you develop daily and weekly planning practices. Here are some weekly habits worth cultivating:

❖ Take 30 minutes on Friday afternoon or Monday morning to plan for the upcoming week (or choose another appropriate time if your workweek follows a different schedule).

❖ Schedule meetings and conversations that will help you move projects forward.

❖ Create a list of decisions you want to make or facilitate and a list of obstacles that need to be overcome. Post the list where you will refer to it daily.

❖ Think about helpful coaching you can offer. Determine at least one skill or situation about which you will seek coaching.

POWER HOUR #10

129

Here are some daily habits worth cultivating:

- ❖ At the beginning of each workday, spend 20 minutes planning.

- ❖ Determine the two or three actions you can take today that will make the greatest difference to your short-term and long-term goals. Do those things.

- ❖ Take a few moments to think about each team member's focus for the day. Is each person working on the most important projects or tasks? What adjustments should you make? What support or coaching would be most helpful? Are there obstacles you collectively need to overcome so each team member can move forward?

- ❖ Plan for your meetings. Meetings are *expensive*! Think about the value of the time of each person sitting around the meeting-room table. Take time at the beginning of each day to plan participation in and leadership of your meeting. When people come to meetings unprepared, they waste time and money. Set the standard and ensure that your meetings are productive and move work forward.

Planning in isolation is not useful. For planning to be most effective, it needs to be combined with regular communication. See the figure below.

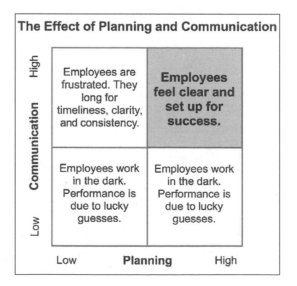

The Effect of Planning and Communication

	Low Planning	High Planning
High Communication	Employees are frustrated. They long for timeliness, clarity, and consistency.	**Employees feel clear and set up for success.**
Low Communication	Employees work in the dark. Performance is due to lucky guesses.	Employees work in the dark. Performance is due to lucky guesses.

Exercise

Each manager should take 10 minutes and begin to fill out the weekly planning checklist. Then, the group should discuss the various sections and the trainer should answer any questions.

Homework/Application Assignment

Do the weekly and daily planning practices for two weeks, communicating regularly with your team and manager.

POWER HOUR 10 Handout ❖ **The Art of Planning**

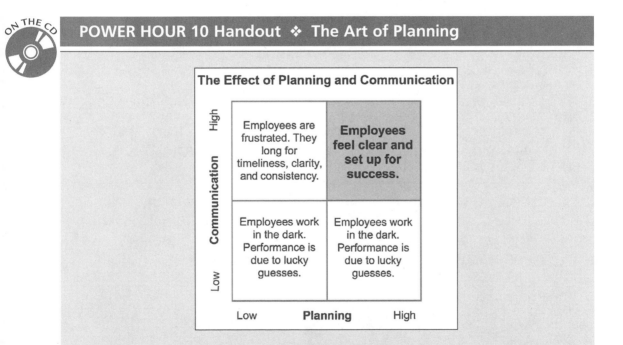

Planning is critical, yet it is done relatively rarely. You can be more focused and successful if you spend just a few minutes each day planning. By definition, planning is not something that has to be done right now, which makes it a perfect target for procrastination. Of course, we all know that this choice will only come back to haunt us later, because a lack of planning means today's urgent tasks are likely to appear unexpectedly.

(continued)

POWER HOUR #10

POWER HOUR 10 Handout ❖ The Art of Planning

Here are some weekly habits worth cultivating:

❖ Take 30 minutes on Friday afternoon or Monday morning to plan for the upcoming week (or choose another appropriate time, if your workweek follows a different schedule).

❖ Schedule meetings and conversations that will help you move things forward.

❖ Create a list of decisions you want to make or facilitate and a list of barriers that need to be obliterated. Post the list where you will refer to it daily.

❖ Think about helpful coaching you can offer. Determine at least one skill or situation about which you will seek coaching.

Here are some daily habits worth cultivating:

❖ At the beginning of each workday spend 20 minutes planning.

❖ Determine the two or three actions you can take today that will make the greatest difference to your short-term and long-term goals. Do those things.

❖ Take a few moments to think about each team member's focus for the day. Is each person working on the most important projects or tasks? What adjustments should you make? What support or coaching would be most helpful? Are there obstacles you need to overcome so team members can move forward?

❖ Plan for your meetings. Meetings are *expensive*! Think about the value of the time of every person sitting around the meeting-room table. Take time at the beginning of each day to plan participation in and leadership of your meeting. When people come to meetings unprepared, they waste time and money. Set the standard and ensure your meetings are productive and move work forward.

(continued)

POWER HOUR #10

POWER HOUR 10 Handout ❖ The Art of Planning

Here are some checklists to help with your daily and weekly planning.

Weekly Planning Checklist

Planning Element	Your Plan for the Week
Gland Slam Home Run for the Week:	
Meetings and conversations I need to schedule:	
Decisions needed and by whom:	
Coaching and developing for the week:	
MUST NOT MISS items:	
Potential barriers to hitting the grand slam for the week:	

Daily Planning Checklist

Planning Element	Your Plan for the Day
Gland Slam Home Run for the Week (*transfer from weekly checklist*):	
Two or three actions that I can make today that will make the greatest difference:	
Team focus; are there any adjustments to be made?	
Barriers I need to obliterate:	
Meetings and prep needed:	

POWER HOUR #10

CHAPTER 17

POWER HOUR 11:
Results-Oriented
Responses

Prework Assignment

Find a brief, current article or blog post to share with people as a warm-up to this Power Hour. It's OK, and preferred, if the piece is provocative or controversial. The prework should stir conversation and prime people for an exploration of the topic.

Learning Objectives

While completing this Power Hour and the application homework, participants will

1. Learn about results-oriented responses

2. Analyze one current situation using the Results-Oriented Response (ROR) cheat sheet

3. Use the ROR cheat sheet to adjust responses for better results.

Trainer's Objective

Produce a one-hour training session that catalyzes great conversations between managers about management.

Agenda

10 Minutes	Brief discussion of prework (and homework if you are doing these in a series, see chapter 4). Pass out the handout.
15 Minutes	Presentation of the conceptual model or topic
10 Minutes	Initial discussion of the concept using provo/evo questions
15 Minutes	Exercise/application
10 Minutes	Final discussion and assignment of homework

Provo/Evo Discussion Questions

1. What does it mean to be results oriented?

2. Is keeping a long to-do list of tasks being result oriented?

3. How do you know that your approach to the situation is helping or hindering your results?

4. Do you sometimes find that you have fallen inactive—or given up—on a frustrating project or task?

Conceptual Model

Sometimes even the hardest working managers need to adjust their approaches to get the best results. Have you ever struggled with a project or task? Results-Oriented Responses, or RORs, are enablers that can have an immediate effect on your work. As you develop your ability to apply RORs in one area, you will also learn skills that will enable you to handle other tasks more effectively. For example, developing dialogue skills for goal setting will also develop your ability to use dialogue to improve processes. An ROR is not a technique itself, but it influences how a technique is used.

Refer to the ROR cheat sheet at the end of this chapter. RORs are listed on the left side of the model and Low Results Responses (LRRs) on the right side. Responses on the left side produce better results. Managers who are dissatisfied with their results can look through this model to find out how to improve their responses.

Exercise

Ask managers to select a project or task that has been giving them problems or where their results are less than they'd like. Give them 10 minutes to read through the ROR cheat sheet and determine whether their responses have been on the left or right side. Ask for a few examples or ideas that came from the exercise.

Homework/Application Assignment

Read through the ROR cheat sheet every morning and whenever you experience a setback or disappointment. Adjust your responses accordingly.

POWER HOUR 11 Handout ❖ **Results-Oriented Responses**

Results-Oriented Responses (ROR) Cheat Sheet

Results-oriented responses (RORs) are listed on the left side of the model and low-results responses (LRRs) on the right side. Responses on the left side produce better results. Managers dissatisfied with their results can look through the model to find out how to improve their responses.

(continued)

POWER HOUR 11 Handout ❖ Results-Oriented Responses

RORs	LRRs
Being an Owner: Assumes responsibility for the outcome. Takes initiative to makes things better. Does whatever it takes to get ideal results. Heart is committed and mind is engaged.	**Being a Custodian**: Does only what is required. Waits for others to act. Hopes someone else will take ownership. Avoids that which is unpleasant. Behavior is compliant. Heart and mind are not fully engaged.
Being Active: Takes the initiative to get things done. Is not easily deterred by setbacks. Proactive. When barriers are present, immediately identifies them and implements an alternative action plan.	**Being Passive**: Won't take action unless told to do so. Acts only when necessary. Reactive in stance and style. Barriers and setbacks result in inaction.
Generating: Able to generate new and better alternative approaches and carry them out. Creates from unlimited possibilities. Does not get stuck on how things are already being done.	**Being Automatic**: Sticks with the way things have always been done, preserves the status quo. Prefers to act by habit and won't move out of his or her comfort zone. Does not create new approaches or solutions.
Keeping Promises: Does what is promised. Fulfills commitments. Keeps his or her word.	**Broken Promises or Commitments**: Does not follow through with what he or she has promised or committed to. Lets to-do items build up beyond the date expected. Does not follow through on real or implied agreements.
Influencing Through Enrollment: Influences others by having them see, understand, and take ownership of the goal for themselves. Demonstrates the strategy and plan in such a way	**Influencing Through Subtle Coercion**: Communicates the vision and plan in a way that resembles a direction or a suggestion. Influences others by making them feel they need to accept

(continued)

POWER HOUR 11 Handout ❖ **Results-Oriented Responses**

RORs	LRRs
that others see and take on the vision for themselves. Others are committed and passionate about the vision and plan.	and conform. This type of influencing rarely results in committed and passionate performance.
Being Service Oriented: Sees his or her role as one that provides service to others. Facilitates cooperation, commitment, and learning. Manages from the mind-set, "What can I do to help others excel today?"	**Expecting to be Served**: Sees his or her role as one in which people should serve him or her. This stance limits the capacity to have impact on others. Manages from the mind-set, "What have you done for me today?"
Being Coachable: Accepts and uses feedback, input, criticism, and ideas from others and is curiously observant. Is not defensive when given feedback. Recognizes that others have something to offer.	**Being Uncoachable**: Blocks the environment from being influential; puts up barriers. Focuses more on being right, looking good, and appearing in charge.
Practicing Quality Dialogue: Communicates with the intent of making a difference or moving a topic forward. Engages in active conversation focused on the topic at hand.	**Using Dialogue Without Purpose**: Communicates in a way that does not move the topic forward. Spends time whining and discussing rumors, gossip, complaints, diversions, and opinions that are not helpful toward enabling the desired result.

CHAPTER 18

POWER HOUR 12: Meetings That Rock!

Prework Assignment

Find a brief, current article or blog post to share with people as a warm-up to this Power Hour. It's OK, and preferred, if the piece is provocative or controversial. The prework should stir conversation and prime people for an exploration of the topic.

Learning Objectives

While completing this Power Hour and the application homework, participants will

1. Discuss the high cost of meetings

2. Identify reasons why and why not to meet

3. Use the meeting planning worksheet to plan an upcoming meeting.

Trainer's Objective

The trainer will produce a one-hour training session that catalyzes great conversations between managers about management.

Agenda

10 Minutes	Brief discussion of prework (and homework if you are doing these in a series; see chapter 4). Pass out the handout.
15 Minutes	Presentation of the conceptual model or topic
10 Minutes	Initial discussion of the concept using provo/evo questions
15 Minutes	Exercise/application
10 Minutes	Final discussion and assignment of homework

Provo/Evo Discussion Questions

1. What percentage of your meetings do you dread? Why?
2. Why do we attend so many meetings?
3. What are some of the alternatives we could use for "update" meetings?
4. What can the meeting leader do to help enliven the business conversation in meetings?

Conceptual Model

Meetings are expensive! Ten people with an average salary of $60,000 per year meet once per week for two hours. The initial cost of this meeting is the participant's time, which comes to about $40,000 per year for this one meeting. The greater price,

POWER HOUR #12

however, is the opportunity costs of the 20 hours per week of time that could be spent on other tasks. If this staff meeting is not a good use of time, it is taking up the equivalent of what a person, working half time, could accomplish. If everyone spends four hours per week in ineffective meetings (the reality is probably much higher), then, for a team of 20, they have lost the equivalent of two full-time employees' worth of work in opportunity costs.

Meetings are conversations. Conversations are your currency for getting work done. Your business conversations will be more effective when the dialogue is healthy, energized, and focused. You spend too much time in meetings not to make sure they are great business discussions. Great business dialogue has seven elements:

- ❖ *Relevance:* The topic of discussion is one that people care about. It makes a difference to their lives.

- ❖ *Inquiry:* Questions are being asked that move the topic forward. The questions are both provocative and evocative.

- ❖ *Freedom:* Participants feel free to openly share their ideas and thoughts, even if those thoughts or ideas are on the fringe.

- ❖ *Connectedness:* There is a sense of shared purpose or interest. The participants feel connected to one another.

- ❖ *Reception:* Participants listen well, interpret the information, provide feedback, and reinforce contribution.

- ❖ *Empowerment:* People feel as though they can have some impact on the topic being discussed. This would ideally mean they can move the problem or opportunity forward, but it could also mean they can move the intellectual debate further.

- ❖ *Play:* The conversation is fun and full of energy. The dialogue has a dynamic that flows and can be playful.

Meetings have become such a staple in modern business that we tend to overuse them. The result is that your schedules become clogged with meetings, leaving little time for other tasks. To ensure that you are making the best use of your and your team members' time, it is important to schedule meetings only when needed.

Meetings should serve one of these purposes:

❖ To obtain feedback, input, or ideas about an important business project, initiative, or problem.

❖ To present recommendations and obtain a decision where a group consensus or agreement is important.

❖ To actively communicate project status where gaining agreement and focus as a group is important (and where a huddle is not sufficient).

Meetings aren't necessary in these cases:

❖ If they provide an update when other communication methods (e.g., email, collaborative project programs, phone, informal discussions, huddles) would be adequate.

❖ If you are not seeking input or do not wish to generate dialogue.

❖ As the default way to communicate. We are too quick to schedule meetings and fill up people's calendars.

In an effort to be inclusive and open, we sometimes invite too many people to our meetings. Although it is nice to have the entire team at every meeting, this is probably overkill. Don't invite people just to keep them in the loop (the equivalent of email's "cc" or FYI). We need to respect the value of people's time and find other ways to keep them informed.

You invite people to meet with you so that they can contribute to the conversation. Make sure your meeting participants know why they have been invited and have any specific information you would like them to bring. Take your role as a meeting participant seriously, too. If you are going to spend several hours a day in meetings, make sure the time is focused and fruitful. The sidebar itemizes meeting expectations for participants (and those who call the meetings!).

> ## *Meeting Expectations for Participants*
>
> ✓ Prepare to participate. Think about the agenda and prepare your thoughts and materials. Ask the meeting leader to clarify desired outcomes if needed.
>
> ✓ Be on time!
>
> ✓ Participate in the discussion. Don't over-participate, though, and take over the conversation.
>
> ✓ Help the meeting stay focused and on track. Help the meeting leader accomplish his or her objectives.
>
> ✓ Follow up on action items assigned to you.

Remember that the purpose of meeting to have an effective business conversation that accomplishes your desired outcomes. If you are the meeting leader, it is your responsibility to ensure that the conversation is worth the time and resources spent. If you are a participant, it is your responsibility to actively participate and contribute to the meeting's focus and success.

Exercise

Ask managers to use the meeting planning worksheet to plan an upcoming meeting. Give them 10 minutes, then ask for feedback or questions.

Homework/Application Assignment

Don't attend bad meetings, and certainly don't schedule them. Use the planning worksheet to help improve business conversations during meetings—beginning with your next meeting.

POWER HOUR 12 Handout ❖ Meetings That Rock!

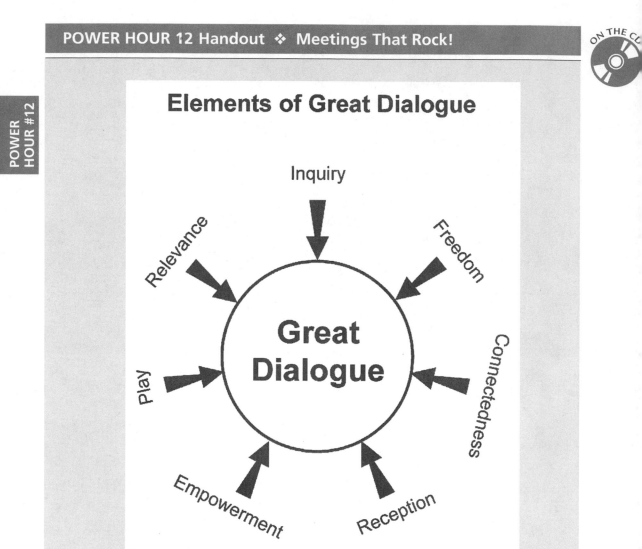

Elements of Great Dialogue

Inquiry

Relevance

Freedom

Great Dialogue

Play

Connectedness

Empowerment

Reception

Meetings should serve one of the following purposes:

❖ To obtain feedback, input, or ideas about an important business project, initiative, or problem.

❖ To present recommendations and obtain a decision where a group consensus or agreement is important.

❖ To actively communicate project status where gaining agreement and focus as a group is important (and where a huddle is not sufficient).

(continued)

POWER HOUR 12 Handout ❖ **Meetings That Rock!**

Meetings aren't necessary in these cases:

❖ If they provide an update when other communication methods (e.g., email, collaborative project programs, phone, informal discussions, huddles) would be adequate.

❖ If you are not seeking input or do not wish to generate dialogue.

❖ As the default way to communicate. We are too quick to schedule meetings and fill up people's calendars.

Meeting Planning Worksheet

Topic: _____

Note: Be sure you focus on one task, problem, opportunity, or a portion of these. Can you create excellent dialogue around this one topic in the time you have available?

Facilitator: Is a facilitator needed? If so, make arrangements and review this worksheet with him or her before the meeting is scheduled.

Desired Outcomes: What do you want to accomplish by the end of this meeting?

1. _____

2. _____

Inquiry: List five provocative or evocative questions that will promote engagement and focused dialogue.

1. _____

2. _____

3. _____

4. _____

5. _____

(continued)

POWER HOUR 12 Handout ❖ Meetings That Rock!

Participants: Who can best contribute to this topic?

1. _____   6. _____

2. _____   7. _____

3. _____   8. _____

4. _____   9. _____

5. _____   10. _____

Invite: Send invitations to the participants and share the topic, desired outcomes, and the five questions you detailed here. If possible, allow at least 48 hours of preparation time.

Prep: Ensure that you set up the meeting room and post or hand out the topic, desired outcomes, and questions. If you need to participate in the discussion, consider asking a trainer or peer to facilitate.

During the Meeting: Periodically check to make sure the conversation is on topic. If necessary, remind participants about the desired outcomes. Manage over-participators and ensure everyone is heard. Encourage and appreciate opposing views. Address what's *not* being said. Take good notes. Offer food and drinks if the meeting will run longer than 90 minutes.

After the Meeting: Thank participants for their input and act on the information they provide. Responsiveness is the best thanks. Communicate changes or progress to ensure everyone is clear (use a huddle, email, internal blog, or other communication vehicle).

Complete _____

CHAPTER 19

POWER HOUR 13: Mastering Your Time

Prework Assignment

Find a brief, current article or blog post to share with people as a warm-up to this Power Hour. It's OK, and preferred, if the piece is provocative or controversial. The prework should stir conversation and prime people for an exploration of the topic.

Learning Objectives

While completing this Power Hour and the application homework, participants will

1. Discuss the problems inherent in multitasking

2. Learn about the technique of "chunking"

3. Give chunking a try for two weeks.

Trainer's Objective

Trainers will produce a one-hour training session that catalyzes great conversations between managers about management.

Agenda

10 Minutes	Brief discussion of prework (and homework if you are doing these in a series; see chapter 4). Pass out the handout.
15 Minutes	Presentation of the conceptual model or topic
10 Minutes	Initial discussion of the concept using provo/evo questions
15 Minutes	Exercise/application
10 Minutes	Final discussion and assignment of homework

Provo/Evo Discussion Questions

1. Is multitasking good or bad?

2. Is multitasking an expectation?

3. How much is your productivity reduced by constant interruptions? What are the key culprits?

4. What have you done to manage and reduce work interruptions?

Conceptual Model

In most companies, the pace of work is hectic and spastic. Managers juggle myriad projects and tasks at the same time. Multitasking, or trying to do many things at once, has become the norm. Unfortunately, multitasking is not the solution for coping with numerous priorities—instead, it wrecks focus and productivity. Managers want to do more with less, but when they multitask, they end up doing less with less. When their attention is jolted from one thing to the next, they lose time during the interruption and even more time as they get back up to speed and return to the task. *If managers are interrupted several times an hour, they end up losing a couple of hours every day.* To perform at your best, you need to learn to focus your resources.

Multitasking wastes time, energy, and concentration, but it is a natural outcrop of today's busy work environment and broader job descriptions. You are not going to change these things overnight, but you can begin to help yourself and your employees achieve greater focus and productivity by implementing chunking. Chunking means carving out segments of time to focus on one thing. This technique helps managers focus and also be responsive.

POWER HOUR #13

You should strive to schedule and enjoy several focusing chunks per week. To enjoy the benefits of chunking, you will need to schedule time chunks in advance and exercise resolve to ensure these precious time blocks do not get consumed by interruptions or diversions. Turn off your cell phone, set your office phone to take messages, and shut down email. Let your team members and colleagues know you need to focus. For that precious period of time, you want to direct all your energies and thoughts to one task, plan, or project. Chunking combines the benefits of focusing on one thing with the need for workers to do various tasks during the day.

Do you find it difficult to disconnect for two to four hours? Imagine you are in a meeting. You can't answer email messages or phone calls (or you shouldn't) at that time. Talk to your staff and make sure they know when you have set aside chunks. Encourage them to do the same and help them rearrange their day to enable chunking. Make chunking a regular practice, and you will find that people get used to it. They learn when to engage one another and when to allow them to focus.

Exercise

Consider your schedule for the next week and decide which projects or tasks are most important to you. Identify two or three times you could set aside as chunks. Write down these times and schedule them like meetings (or do so once you return to your desk). Allow five minutes for individuals to select times, then discuss the ideas they have for how to give chunking a try— how will they ensure they are not interrupted?

Homework/Application Assignment

Give chunking a try over the next two weeks. Block off at least one chunk per day.

POWER HOUR 13 Handout ❖ Mastering Your Time

In most companies, the pace of work is hectic and spastic. Managers juggle myriad projects and tasks at the same time. Multitasking, or trying to do many things at once, has become the norm. Unfortunately, multitasking is not the solution for coping with numerous priorities—instead, it wrecks focus and productivity. Managers want to do more with less, but when they multitask, they end up doing less with less. When their attention is jolted from one thing to the next, they lose time during the interruption and take more time to get back up to speed and return to the task. *If managers are interrupted several times an hour, they end up losing a couple of hours every day.* To perform at your best, you need to learn to focus your resources.

Multitasking wastes time, energy, and concentration, but it is a natural outcrop of today's busy work environment and broader job descriptions. You are not going to change these things overnight, but you can begin helping yourself and your employees achieve greater focus and productivity by implementing chunking. Chunking helps managers focus and also be responsive. Chunking means carving out segments of time that you will use to focus on one thing. You should strive to schedule and enjoy several focusing chunks per week. To enjoy the benefits of chunking, you will need to schedule time chunks in advance and exercise resolve to ensure these precious time blocks do not get consumed by interruptions or diversions. Turn off your cell phone, set your office

POWER HOUR 13 Handout ❖ **Mastering Your Time**

phone to take messages, and shut down email. Let your team members and colleagues know you need to focus. For that precious period of time, you want to direct all your energies and thoughts to one task, plan, or project. Chunking combines the benefits of focusing on one thing with the need for workers to do various tasks during the day.

Do you find it difficult to disconnect for two to four hours? Imagine you are in a meeting. You can't answer email messages or phone calls (or at least you shouldn't!) at that time. Talk to your staff and make sure they know when you have set aside chunks. Encourage them to do the same and help them rearrange their day to enable chunking. Make chunking a regular practice, and you will find that people get used to it. They learn when to engage one another and when to allow them to focus.

The table shows a sample chunking schedule:

Day	Early Morning	Late Morning	Early Afternoon	Late Afternoon
Monday	8:00–10:00		1:00–2:00	
Tuesday	8:00–9:00		1:00–2:00	2:00–4:00
Wednesday	8:00–9:00		1:00–2:00	
Thursday	8:00–9:00		1:00–2:00	
Friday	8:00–9:00		1:00–2:00	2:00–4:00

CHAPTER 20

POWER HOUR 14:
Internal Service Excellence

Prework Assignment

Find a brief, current article or blog post to share with people as a warm-up to this Power Hour. It's OK, and preferred, if the piece is provocative or controversial. The prework should stir conversation and prime people for an exploration of the topic.

Learning Objectives

While completing this Power Hour and the application homework, participants will

1. Discuss the importance of internal customer service excellence

2. Identify key indicators of service excellence

3. Hold a meeting to discuss internal service excellence with team members and internal customers.

Trainer's Objective

Trainers will produce a one-hour training session that catalyzes great conversations between managers about management.

Agenda:

10 Minutes	Brief discussion of prework (and homework if you are doing these in a series; see chapter 4). Pass out the handout.
15 Minutes	Presentation of the conceptual model or topic
10 Minutes	Initial discussion of the concept using provo/evo questions
15 Minutes	Exercise/application
10 Minutes	Final discussion and assignment of homework

Provo/Evo Discussion Questions

1. To what degree is the definition of service excellence known and shared?

2. If your yearly bonus or raise was determined by the grade your internal customers gave you, how well would you do?

3. Do you define your success and results from the perspective of the supplier or the customer? What about internal customers?

Conceptual Model

As managers, you have internal customers whom you must satisfy. Sometimes the needs and desires of internal customers are not adequately considered when we set goals or establish priorities and metrics. You and your department are also internal customers: Do you feel well served? It is important to define internal service excellence.

What does service excellence look like during meetings? What does service excellence look like when it comes to solving problems? What does service excellence look like when it comes to improving processes? What does service excellence look like in terms of collaboration? What does service excellence look like with regard to how much or how little hassle people experience?

Here are some assumptions you can make:

✓ Your customer relations can only be as good as your internal relations with one another.

✓ Your internal relationships are built and reinforced through communication.

✓ Communication occurs in conversations—in person, on the phone, in writing, in meetings.

✓ Your customer relations can only be as good as the conversations you have with one another.

Service excellence starts inside the organization and is a reflection of the strength of your relationships. Often, we are not aware of the strengths and weaknesses of our internal service. To determine how internal service excellence looks, do these things:

❖ Think about what you expect and hope for as an internal customer.

❖ Think about the requests you get from your internal customers.

❖ The manager–employee relationship is both customer and supplier. The manager serves (is a supplier for) his or her employees (who are customers) and employees serve (are suppliers for) their manager (who is a customer). How well are you serving your employees?

❖ Define service excellence in terms of how effective service and support looks and feels to you.

POWER HOUR #14

❖ Think about what you expect and hope for when you are a customer of similar services.

❖ Think about the company's mission and goals and how internal service supports these goals.

How would your goals and priorities change if you explored these topics with your team and internal customers? How should your work change to better meet internal customer expectations?

Exercise

Working in small groups, come up with a short list of ways in which managers can better define internal service excellence. What can and should you each be doing to ensure that you and your teams are meeting internal customer expectations? Allow 10 minutes for the work, then ask for examples.

Homework/Application Assignment

Dedicate an upcoming staff meeting to the discussion of internal customer service excellence. Invite key internal customers to be a part of the conversation. Adjust your practices and processes as necessary.

POWER HOUR 14 Handout ❖ Internal Service Excellence

As managers, you have internal customers whom you must satisfy. Sometimes the needs and desires of internal customers are not adequately considered when setting goals or establishing priorities and metrics. You and your department are also internal customers—do you feel well served? It is important to define internal service excellence.

What does service excellence look like during meetings? What does service excellence look like when it comes to solving problems? What does service excellence look like when it comes to improving processes? What does service excellence look like in terms of collaboration? What does service excellence look like with regard to how much or how little hassle people experience?

(continued)

POWER HOUR 14 Handout ❖ **Internal Service Excellence**

Here are some assumptions you can make:

✓ Your customer relations can only be as good as your internal relations with one another.

✓ Your internal relationships are built and reinforced through communication.

✓ Communication occurs in conversations—in person, on the phone, in writing, in meetings.

✓ Your customer relations can only be as good as the conversations you have with one another.

Service excellence starts inside the organization and is a reflection of the strength of your relationships. Often, we are not aware of the strengths and weaknesses of our internal service. To determine how internal service excellence looks, we must do these things:

❖ Think about what you expect and hope for as an internal customer.

❖ Think about the requests you get from your internal customers.

❖ The manager–employee relationship is both customer and supplier. The manager serves (is a supplier for) his or her employees (who are customers), and employees serve (are suppliers for) their manager (who is a customer). How well are you serving your employees?

❖ Define service excellence in terms of how effective service and support looks and feels to you.

❖ Think about what you expect and hope for when you are a customer of similar services.

❖ Think about the company's mission and goals and how internal service supports these goals.

How would your goals and priorities change if you explored these topics with your team and internal customers? How should your work change to better meet internal customer expectations?

CHAPTER 21

POWER HOUR 15: Your Leadership Legacy

Prework Assignment

Find a brief, current article or blog post to share with people as a warm-up to this Power Hour. It's OK, and preferred, if the piece is provocative or controversial. The prework should stir conversation and prime people for an exploration of the topic.

Learning Objectives

While completing this Power Hour and the application homework, participants will

1. Discuss the importance of their managerial legacy

2. Identify one aspect of their desired legacy

3. Define and communicate what they want to be known for and how they wish to be regarded.

Trainer's Objective

Trainers will produce a one-hour training session that catalyzes great conversations between managers about management.

Agenda

10 Minutes	Brief discussion of prework (and homework if you are doing these in a series; see chapter 4). Pass out the handout.
15 Minutes	Presentation of the conceptual model or topic
10 Minutes	Initial discussion of the concept using provo/evo questions
15 Minutes	Exercise/application
10 Minutes	Final discussion and assignment of homework

Provo/Evo Discussion Questions

1. If you were hit by a bus today, or decided to move to Tahiti, what would you be known for?

2. When you move on to whatever is next, how do you want to be remembered?

3. Think about the best and worst bosses you have had. Do you think that either person was aware of his or her legacy?

4. If you work hard and do good work, should you care about how people remember you?

Conceptual Model

What kind of a legacy would you like to leave? Is there a particular project that you want to be known for? Would you like

POWER HOUR #15

to create an amazing team? Do you want to revolutionize the way your company plans for innovation? Do you want to lead record-breaking gains in financial performance? Imagine that you are a fly in the elevator one week after you leave. Two people are talking about you. What would you like to hear them say? All managers should think about the legacy they wish to leave. Creating a vision of your legacy for yourself will help shape your actions and results today and in the future.

In addition to the broad or grand accomplishments you seek, think about the ways in which you want to be known as a role model. Do you want to be known as the queen of exciting meetings or the king of provocative analysis? Do you want to be known for always being organized and prepared? Creative and innovative? Fun? Think about what you want to be known for and the type of reputation you seek to build.

We are creating our legacy every day. That's why we need to think about it now. You may not retire or move on for several years, but your actions and words today are what will determine the impact you have in the organization. Defining your legacy is not driven by a need to please others but rather by the opportunity to determine the type and size of the contribution you will make.

Exercise

Write down one result or quality for which you want to be known. Honestly assess to what degree you are performing at the level you desire on a scale of 1–10, 10 being "I'm doing this today." Give managers five minutes to work, then ask them to share their quality and self-assessment.

Homework/Application Assignment

Define the legacy you want to leave, and communicate this with your manager and team.

POWER HOUR #15

POWER HOUR 15 Handout ❖ **Your Leadership Legacy**

What kind of a legacy would you like to leave? Is there a particular project that you want to be known for? Would you like to create an amazing team? Do you want to revolutionize the way your company plans for innovation? Do you want to lead record-breaking gains in financial performance? Imagine that you are a fly in the elevator one week after you leave. Two people are talking about you. What would you like to hear them say? All managers should think about the legacy they wish to leave. Creating a vision of your own legacy will help shape your actions and results today and in the future.

In addition to the broad or grand accomplishments you seek, think about the ways in which you want to be known as a role model. Do you want to be known as the queen of exciting meetings or the king of provocative analysis? Do you want to be known for always being organized and prepared? Creative and innovative? Fun? Think about for what you want to be known and the type of reputation you seek to build.

We are creating our legacy every day. That's why we need to think about it now. You may not retire or move on for several years, but your actions and words today are what will determine the impact you have in the organization. Defining your legacy is not driven by the need to please others but rather by the opportunity to determine the type and size of the contribution you will make.

Aspects of Management	The Legacy You Want to Leave
Results and contribution to the business	
Team health and development	
Peer partnership and collaboration	
Creativity and innovation	
Processes and practices	
The workplace culture	
Systems and structure	
Change and agility	

POWER HOUR #15

CHAPTER 22

POWER HOUR 16: Knowing When and How to Say "No"

Prework Assignment

Find a brief, current article or blog post to share with people as a warm-up to this Power Hour. It's OK, and preferred, if the piece is provocative or controversial. The prework should stir conversation and prime people for an exploration of the topic.

Learning Objectives

While completing this Power Hour and the application homework, participants will

1. Discuss the importance of saying "No"

2. Identify two tasks to which they should say "No."

3. Negotiate these two items within a week of the training.

Trainer's Objective

The trainer will produce a one-hour training session that catalyzes great conversations between managers about management.

Agenda

10 Minutes	Brief discussion of prework (and homework if you are doing these in a series; see chapter 4). Pass out the handout.
15 Minutes	Presentation of the conceptual model or topic
10 Minutes	Initial discussion of the concept using provo/evo questions
15 Minutes	Exercise/application
10 Minutes	Final discussion and assignment of homework

Provo/Evo Discussion Questions

1. Do you say "Yes" or "No" too much? Which? Why?

2. Which does our culture reinforce—"Yes" managers or "No" managers?

3. What's the best way you know how to say "No"?

4. Should managers be afraid to say "No"?

5. Regardless of fear or culture, are managers obligated to say "No"?

Conceptual Model

Managers need to say "No" to wrong things and even to many good things. Saying "No" can improve focus. When you first begin to say "No," expect a puzzled reaction. Stick with it, though: Once people see how well you can focus, they will understand and may even follow suit. (Wouldn't that be nice?) Here are seven common opportunities to improve focus by saying "No":

1. *When you don't think you should attend a meeting.* Talk to the meeting leader and make it clear that your first priority right now is (whatever it happens to be). Reinforce that you would be happy to be on call for any issues that come up and need your input.

2. *When meetings are not effective.* Be honest and resolve to not sit through another bad meeting. Share your observations with the group. Acknowledge that everyone is busy and you are concerned that this meeting is not a good use of time. Request that the meeting agenda be changed, the frequency of these meetings reduced, or the meetings be canceled altogether. Organizations have many ways to keep people in the loop. If your manager is the meeting leader, have a private conversation before the meeting. Chances are, your manager is feeling the same way.

3. *Someone is proposing new tasks or projects that you don't think deserve the resources required.* Ask the individual or team considering this work whether this task, relative to everything else going on, will make a big difference to the company's goals. If they say the task should be top priority, ask what project should then be taken off the priority list to compensate.

4. *Your manager wants everyone to do new detailed weekly reports and you think this is a waste of time.* Ask your manager what unfilled need the report will serve. Make it clear that you are concerned about spending time to document detailed activities instead of doing them, and ask if there are other ways that you could meet the need. Often, you will be able to get your manager to compromise a bit.

POWER HOUR #16

5. *You have been asked to check out an idea from a recent trade magazine article.* Let the requestor know that, although it sounds interesting, you do not want to get sidetracked or distracted from your focus this week. Offer to ask an intern to do some research when there's time, but make no commitments as to when this will be. Often, the requestor will just drop the idea.

6. *You have been asked to do something and you don't feel you are the right person for the task.* Poor role clarity, delegation, and empowerment can wreck focus. Talk to the person about why you do not think that you or your team members are the appropriate persons for this task.

7. *You have been asked to multitask during a time that you need to focus.* Focus time is precious time! Although emergencies may occur, protect your time from everyday interruptions (especially from chatting—the most common interruption!) by nicely asking people if you can chat later and letting them know when you will be available.

Beware of these wimpy ways to say "No." Avoid them all, as they will make you seem weak and unsure of yourself.

✓ *"I am not taking on new responsibilities."* This is a weak reponse because you *would* add a high-priority task to your list if you were asked to. Don't say this when what you really mean is, "This task is not important."

✓ *"I don't have room on my calendar."* This is a weak response because it speaks more to your inability to manage your calendar than to do the task. If the task were important, you would make room on your calendar.

✓ *"I cannot do this now, but I can do it later."* This might be weak if it is just an excuse to avoid a confrontation about the task. If the task is not a good use of time, don't offer to do it later. If the task is a good use of your time, then go ahead—but be clear about when you can complete it.

It is every manager's responsibility to say "No." The better you get at being open and clear about the tasks and projects you and your team should *not* be working on, the better your focus and results will be.

Exercise

Ask managers to write down two things currently on their to-do lists or work plans to which they should say "No" and to identify the persons with whom they ought to discuss the tasks. Give them five minutes to identify the two items, then ask for examples.

Homework/Application Assignment

Within the next week, negotiate at least the two items you identified during this session. Say "No" at least twice this week. Give kudos to a team member or peer who says "No."

POWER HOUR 16 Handout ❖ **Knowing When and How to Say "No"**

Managers need to say "No" to wrong things and even to many good things. Saying "No" improves focus. When you first start saying "No," expect a puzzled reaction. Stick with it, though: Once people see how well you can focus, they will understand and may even follow suit. (Wouldn't that be nice?) Here are seven common opportunities to improve focus by saying, "No":

✓ **When you don't think you should attend a meeting.** Talk to the meeting leader and make it clear that your first priority right now is (whatever it happens to be). Reinforce that you would be happy to be on call for any issues that come up and that need your input.

✓ **When meetings are not effective.** Be honest and resolve to not sit through another bad meeting. Share your observations with the group. Acknowledge that everyone is busy and you are concerned that this meeting is not a good use of time. Request that the meeting agenda be changed, the frequency of these meetings reduced, or the meetings be canceled altogether. Organizations have many

(continued)

POWER HOUR #16

169

POWER HOUR 16 Handout ❖ Knowing When and How to Say "No"

ways to keep people in the loop. If your manager is the meeting leader, have a private conversation before the meeting. Chances are, your manager is feeling the same way.

✓ **Someone is proposing new tasks or projects that you don't think deserve the resources requir**ed. Ask the individual or team considering this work whether this task, relative to everything else going on, will make a big difference to the company's goals. If they say the task should be top priority, ask what project should be taken off the priority list to compensate.

✓ **Your manager wants everyone to do new detailed weekly reports, and you think this is a waste of time.** Ask your manager what unfilled need the report will serve. Make it clear that you are concerned about spending time to document detailed activities instead of doing them, and ask if there are other ways that you could meet the need. Often, you will be able to get your manager to compromise a bit.

✓ **You have been asked to check out an idea from a recent trade magazine article.** Let the requestor know that, although it sounds interesting, you do not want to get sidetracked or distracted from your focus this week. Offer to ask an intern to do some research when there's time, but make no commitment as to when this will be. Often, the requestor will just drop the idea.

✓ **You have been asked to do something and you don't feel you are the right person for the task.** Poor role clarity, delegation, and empowerment can wreck focus. Talk to the person about why you do not think that you or your team members are the appropriate persons for this task.

✓ **You have been asked to multitask during a time that you need to focus.** Focus time is precious time! Although emergencies may occur, protect your time from everyday interruptions (especially from chatting—the most common interruption!) by nicely asking people

(continued)

POWER HOUR 16 Handout ❖ **Knowing When and How to Say "No"**

if you can chat later and letting them know when you will be available.

Beware of these wimpy ways to say no. Avoid them all, as they will make you seem weak and unsure of yourself:

✓ **"I am not taking on new responsibilities."** This is a weak response, because you *would* add a high-priority task to your list. Don't say this when what you really mean is, "This task is not important."

✓ **"I don't have room on my calendar."** This is a weak response, because it speaks more to your inability to manage your calendar than to do the task. If the task were important, you would make room on your calendar.

✓ **"I cannot do this now, but I can do it later."** This might be weak if it is just an excuse to avoid a confrontation about the task. If the task is not a good use of time, don't offer to do it later. If the task is a good use of your time, then go ahead—but be clear about when you can complete it.

It is every manager's responsibility to say "No." The better you get at being open and clear about the tasks and projects you and your team should *not* be working on, the better your focus and results will be.

POWER HOUR #16

171

CHAPTER 23

POWER HOUR 17: Aligning Your Department for Success

Prework Assignment

Find a brief, current article or blog post to share with people as a warm-up to this Power Hour. It's OK, and preferred, if the piece is provocative or controversial. The prework should stir conversation and prime people for an exploration of the topic.

Learning Objectives

While completing this Power Hour and the application homework, participants will

1. Discuss the importance of alignment

2. Complete a cursory alignment analysis relative to one departmental goal

3. Meet with their team to discuss alignment and how they can be better set up for success.

Trainer's Objective

Trainers will produce a one-hour training session that catalyzes great conversations between managers about management.

Agenda

10 Minutes	Brief discussion of prework (and homework if you are doing these in a series; see chapter 4). Pass out the handout.
15 Minutes	Presentation of the conceptual model or topic
10 Minutes	Initial discussion of the concept using provo/evo questions
15 Minutes	Exercise/application
10 Minutes	Final discussion and assignment of homework

Provo/Evo Discussion Questions

1. Are you and your team members set up for success? Why or why not?

2. What does lack of alignment feel like? What does it look like?

3. How often do you need to think about alignment?

4. If you could make just one adjustment to better align your department for success, what would that be?

Conceptual Model

A well-aligned department hums with efficiency. Processes for getting the work done are clearly understood and effective. Staff members' roles support the goals of both the team and the company. Individuals are clear about what they should contribute. They are appropriately empowered and held accountable for producing results. Communication to and from departments facilitates each team's ability to remain on course and prioritize. The organizational structure and individual roles enable team members to identify and solve problems quickly. Work is more satisfying because it makes sense.

In contrast, poorly aligned organizational structures and processes cause numerous problems with quality, throughput, and results. When a structure or process is out of alignment with the larger goal it was designed to support, it no longer serves the goals of the team and the company. Poor alignment can occur for various reasons. Perhaps changes have occurred in one area of the organization but not in others. Sometimes the problem is a lack of effective processes for getting the work done, or it could be that roles have changed but processes have not, or vice versa.

A common reason for poor alignment is conflict among technology, processes, and roles. For team members, a poorly aligned organization feels disorganized, and getting work done seems more difficult than it should. Ambiguous, confusing, and overlapping roles are also signs of poor alignment. The design and planning of workflow is significant and should be a major focus for middle managers. Many of them assume, however, that unproductive people are to blame for poor results. Although there may be personnel problems for the manager to resolve, it is more likely that the department's processes and structures are responsible.

Is your department set up for success?

Exercise

Ask participants to write down one major departmental goal for the year. Then ask each to spend five minutes reviewing the Table of Alignment Elements on the backside of their handout to quickly determine if their department is set up for success

POWER HOUR #17

175

relative to this one goal. Allow 10 minutes for the work, then ask for examples.

Homework/Application Assignment

Hold a team meeting to discuss alignment. Show team members the table of alignment elements on the handout and ask for their input about changes that would better enable them to be successful. Do this quarterly and make adjustments as possible and as needed.

POWER HOUR 17 Handout ❖ **Aligning Your Department for Success**

A well-aligned department hums with efficiency. Processes for getting the work done are clearly understood and effective. Staff members' roles support the goals of both the team and company. Individuals are clear about what they should contribute. They are appropriately empowered and held accountable for producing results. Communication to and from departments facilitates each team's ability to remain on course and prioritize. The organizational structure and individual roles enable team members to identify and solve problems quickly. Work is more satisfying because it makes sense.

In contrast, poorly aligned organizational structures and processes cause numerous problems with quality, throughput, and results. When a structure or process is out of alignment with the larger goal it was designed to support, it no longer serves the goals of the team and company. Poor alignment can occur for various reasons. Perhaps changes have occurred in one area of the organization but not in others. Sometimes the problem is a lack of effective processes for getting the work done, or it could be that roles have changed but processes have not, or vice versa.

A common reason for poor alignment is conflict among technology, processes, and roles. For team members, a poorly aligned organization feels disorganized, and getting work done seems more difficult than it should. Ambiguous, confusing, and overlapping roles are also signs of poor alignment. The design and planning of workflow is significant and should be a major focus for middle managers. Many of them assume, however, that unproductive people are to blame for poor results. Although there may be personnel problems for the manager to resolve, it is more likely that the department's processes and structures are responsible for poor results.

Is your department set up for success? Why or why not? Use the following chart to help you decide.

Table of Alignment Elements

Systemic Elements	Aligned for Success	Not Aligned for Success	Why?
Structure			
Culture			
Processes			
Practices			
Goals			
Organization Metrics			
Communication and Decision-Making Processes			
Technology			
Workflow			
Skills			
Management Practices			
Other Element			
Other Element			

POWER HOUR #17

POWER HOUR 18: The Art of Employee One-on-Ones

Prework Assignment

Find a brief, current article or blog post to share with people as a warm-up to this Power Hour. It's OK, and preferred, if the piece is provocative or controversial. The prework should stir conversation and prime people for an exploration of the topic.

Learning Objectives

While completing this Power Hour and the application home-work, participants will

1. Discuss the value of one-on-one meetings

2. Review techniques for improving one-on-one conversations

3. Book and hold one-on-ones with all direct reports within one month of the training.

Trainer's Objective

Trainers will produce a one-hour training session that catalyzes great conversations between managers about management.

Agenda

10 Minutes	Brief discussion of prework (and homework if you are doing these in a series; see chapter 4). Pass out the handout.
15 Minutes	Presentation of the conceptual model or topic
10 Minutes	Initial discussion of the concept using provo/evo questions
15 Minutes	Exercise/application
10 Minutes	Final discussion and assignment of homework

Provo/Evo Discussion Questions

1. Who holds one-on-ones with their employees? How often do you do them?

2. Managers are so busy—are one-on-one meetings practical and worth the time?

3. What makes a one-on-one a good or bad experience?

4. How often do you have a one-on-one with your manager? Do you book him or her for regular one-on-ones? Why or why not?

Conceptual Model

Employee one-on-ones are a managerial tool that can improve dialogue and execution. All managers should have one-on-one meetings with their employees monthly, or as needed.

A one-on-one is a meeting between two people to discuss current and future work. This is not a performance review, but rather a regular business discussion about the work. One-on-ones can also occur between peers, team members, and customers and suppliers. The one-on-one lasts from 30 to 60 minutes and is held weekly, biweekly, or monthly. Here are some topics of discussion typically included:

- ❖ Status of projects
- ❖ Status of assignments and tasks
- ❖ Barriers and roadblocks
- ❖ Changes coming down the pike
- ❖ Goals
- ❖ Development plans
- ❖ Reviews of new procedures or processes
- ❖ Idea sharing
- ❖ Other general Q&A.

Regular one-on-ones have a number of benefits:

- ❖ Improved clarity and focus for all parties involved
- ❖ Faster identification and removal of roadblocks and barriers
- ❖ Improved communication and relationships—better mutual trust and cooperation
- ❖ Improved performance relative to goals
- ❖ Improved execution
- ❖ Improved focus on development and a greater likelihood to follow through with development plans.

POWER HOUR #18

What are the limitations of one-on-ones?

❖ They take time!

❖ Although one-on-ones are held regularly, they should not become substitutions for daily business conversations.

❖ One-on-ones are only as effective as is the conversation. Is it open, candid, and lively?

❖ When one-on-ones are put off and rescheduled, they lose effectiveness. One-on-ones need to be high on the list of priorities.

❖ Some issues and opportunities should be discussed with the entire team.

One-on-ones are often initiated by the manager, but it does not have to be this way. Encourage your employees to book one-on-one meetings with you as needed, in addition to the regular meeting you book with each person.

Here are some ways to make one-on-ones more fruitful, fun, and worthwhile:

✓ *Meet as often as possible and as makes sense.* When one-on-ones are not held often enough, there is too much to cover and the conversation suffers.

✓ *Schedule one-on-ones for a regular time and day each week and try to keep the schedule.* This regimen will ensure that more one-on-ones occur. Hold one-on-ones in a place with few distractions. A meeting room is often better than an office.

✓ *Establish a regular agenda with some time for ad hoc topics.*

✓ *Take notes and send a follow-up email to confirm what was agreed upon.* The email should focus on the assignments and agreements, not the nitty gritty of the conversation.

✓ *Come to the meeting prepared with the information you need to have a good discussion.* Bring reports and examples. Try to resolve as much as possible at the one-on-one.

✓ *Both parties should ask lots of questions and be willing to share fully (as appropriate).* If all you do is go over project and task status, the one-on-one will lack oomph and impact. Managers should ask about barriers, challenges, and ideas. Employees should ask for feedback, relevant changes and news, goal performance, upcoming opportunities, and ideas. Both should ask about how they can help the other succeed. Peers should share challenges and ask about ideas, upcoming changes, barriers, and how they can help one another succeed.

✓ *Periodically, the entire one-on-one should focus on development and career goals.* Although development may be discussed regularly, it is wise to dedicate some time each quarter to the discussion of career goals and development. This may seem most appropriate for the manager–employee one-on-ones, but it would be beneficial for peers to discuss their goals, as well. Peers can often help each other broaden their skills and experiences.

✓ *Take time to brainstorm new ideas.* Have fun with this! If sharing new ideas is a regular part of the agenda, both parties are more likely to come to the table with ideas to share.

Exercise

Ask the managers to create a meeting agenda for their next one-on-ones with their own managers, using the suggestions from the handout. Encourage them to book a one-on-one if one is not scheduled in the next two weeks. Give them 10 minutes to work on their agendas, then ask for a couple of volunteers to share one or two of their questions.

POWER HOUR #18

Homework/Application Assignment

Schedule and conduct employee one-on-ones with each of your direct reports within the next month.

POWER HOUR 18 Handout ❖ The Art of Employee One-on-Ones

Employee one-on-ones are a managerial tool that can improve dialogue and execution. All managers should have one-on-one meetings with their employees monthly or as needed.

A one-on-one is a meeting between two people to discuss current and future work. This is not a performance review, but rather a regular business discussion about the work. One-on-ones can also occur between peers, team members, and customers and suppliers. The one-on-one lasts from 30 to 60 minutes and is held weekly, biweekly, or monthly.

Here are some topics of discussion typically included:

- ❖ Status of projects
- ❖ Status of assignments and tasks
- ❖ Barriers and roadblocks
- ❖ Changes on the horizon
- ❖ Goals
- ❖ Development plans
- ❖ Reviews of new procedures or processes
- ❖ Idea sharing
- ❖ Other general Q&A.

Regular one-on-ones have several benefits:

- ❖ Improved clarity and focus for all parties involved
- ❖ Faster identification and removal of roadblocks and barriers
- ❖ Improved communication and relationships—better mutual trust and cooperation
- ❖ Improved performance relative to goals
- ❖ Improved execution
- ❖ Improved focus on development and a greater likelihood to follow through with development plans.

(continued)

POWER HOUR #18

POWER HOUR 18 Handout ❖ The Art of Employee One-on-Ones

What are the limitations of one-on-ones?

- ❖ They take time!
- ❖ Although one-on-ones are held regularly, they should not become substitutions for daily business conversations.
- ❖ One-on-ones are only as effective as is the conversation. Is it open, candid and lively?
- ❖ When one-on-ones are put off and rescheduled, they lose effectiveness. One-on-ones need to be high on the list of priorities.
- ❖ Some issues and opportunities should be discussed with the entire team.

One-on-ones are often initiated by the manager, but it does not have to be this way. Encourage your employees to book one-on-one meetings with you as needed, in addition to the regular meeting you book with each person.

Here are some ways to make one-on-ones more fruitful, fun, and worthwhile:

- ✓ **Meet as often as possible and as makes sense.** When one-on-ones are not held often enough, there is too much to cover and the conversation suffers.

- ✓ **Schedule one-on-ones for a regular time and day each week, and try to keep the schedule.** This regimen will ensure that more one-on-ones occur. Hold one-on-ones in a place with few distractions. A meeting room is often better than an office.

- ✓ **Establish a regular agenda with some time for ad hoc topics.**

- ✓ **Take notes and send a follow-up email to confirm what was agreed to.** The email should focus on the assignments and agreements, not the nitty gritty of the conversation.

- ✓ **Come to the meeting prepared with the information you need to have a good discussion.** Bring reports and examples. Try to resolve as much as possible at the one-on-one.

(continued)

POWER HOUR 18 Handout ❖ The Art of Employee One-on-Ones

✓ **Both parties should ask lots of questions and be willing to share fully (as appropriate).** If all you do is go over project and task status, the one-on-one will lack oomph and impact. Managers should ask about barriers, challenges, and ideas. Employees should ask for feedback, relevant changes and news, goal performance, upcoming opportunities, and ideas. Both should ask about how they can help the other succeed. Peers should share challenges and ask about ideas, upcoming changes, barriers, and how they can help other succeed.

✓ **Periodically, the entire one-on-one should focus on development and career goals**. Although development may be discussed regularly, it is wise to dedicate some time each quarter to the discussion of career goals and development. This may seem most appropriate for the manager–employee one-on-ones, but it would be beneficial for peers to discuss their goals, as well. Peers can often help each other broaden their skills and experiences.

✓ **Take time to brainstorm new ideas.** Have fun with this! If sharing new ideas is a regular part of the agenda, both parties are more likely to come to the table with ideas to share.

CHAPTER 25

POWER HOUR 19: Enlivening Minds at Work

Prework Assignment

Find a brief, current article or blog post to share with people as a warm-up to this Power Hour. It's OK, and preferred, if the piece is provocative or controversial. The prework should stir conversation and prime people for an exploration of the topic.

Learning Objectives

While completing this Power Hour and the application homework, participants will

1. Discuss the importance of enlivening minds at work

2. Identify key enablers and barriers to employee engagement

3. Create a plan to improve engagement in the coming week.

Trainer's Objective

Produce a one-hour training session that catalyzes great conversations between managers about management.

Agenda

10 Minutes	Brief discussion of prework (and homework if you are doing these in a series; see chapter 4). Pass out the handout.
15 Minutes	Presentation of the conceptual model or topic
10 Minutes	Initial discussion of the concept using provo/evo questions
15 Minutes	Exercise/application
10 Minutes	Final discussion and assignment of homework

Provo/Evo Discussion Questions

1. What does an enlivened mind look like at work?

2. How can we tell if our employees are engaged?

3. What are some of the causes of disengagement?

3. Do you know your employees' natural strengths? What percentage of time do they get to play to their strengths at work?

Conceptual Model

What purpose does a team serve? Why is a team structure of any advantage? Why don't we just have individual contributors who do their own thing? The only reason to have a team and to develop a team is to benefit from members' abilities to think and work together, to strengthen interest and commitment, and thereby to make the organization stronger and more successful. That's it—that's why we have teams. As team managers, we need to ensure that team members do great work together. Team work is a social act, just like management is a social act. The work of teams occurs in conversation—all teams can do is think, collaborate, decide, and coordinate or plan. And it all starts with good thinking and enlivened minds.

Intelligent, hard-working people sometimes perform far below their potential. Many times, this can be attributed to burnout or the person being in the wrong job. Most of the time, however, it's a management problem. The degree to which our team members' minds are engaged in their work is a direct reflection of our management effectiveness—largely a function of how well we connect with our employees and utilize their strengths. In other words, it's our fault, either way. Individuals might get into a funk every now and then, and this is normal. If you have people on your team who are just going through the motions, though, you have a systemic management challenge.

Enlivening minds begins with role modeling. Is your mind alive and engaged? If not, you need to fix this post haste, because no one wants to get excited about working for an uninspired manager.

Exercise

Split the group into subgroups of three or four. Ask each group to take 10 minutes to brainstorm a list of things managers can do to enliven minds at work. Ask each group to share its lists.

Homework/Application Assignment

Over the next week, do two or three things specifically to improve team member engagement.

POWER HOUR #19

189

POWER HOUR 19 Handout ❖ Enlivening Minds at Work

What purpose does a team serve? Why is a team structure of any advantage? Why don't we just have individual contributors who do their own thing? The only reason to have a team and to develop a team is to benefit from members' abilities to think and work together, to strengthen interest and commitment, and thereby to make the organization stronger and more successful. That's it—that's why we have teams. As team managers, we need to ensure that team members do great work together. Team work is a social act, just like management is a social act. The work of teams occurs in conversation—all teams can do is think, collaborate, decide, and coordinate or plan. And it all starts with good thinking and enlivened minds.

Intelligent, hard-working people sometimes perform far below their potential. Many times, this is attributable to burnout or the person being in the wrong job. Most of the time, however, it's a management problem. The degree that our team members' minds are engaged in their work is a direct reflection of our management effectiveness—largely a function of how well we connect with our employees and utilize their strengths. In other words, it's our fault, either way. Individuals might get into a funk every now and then, and this is normal. If you have people on your team who are just going through the motions, though, you have a systemic management challenge.

Enlivening minds begins with role modeling. Is your mind alive and engaged? If not, you need to fix this post haste, because no one wants to get excited about working for an uninspired manager.

To Enliven...	Try This...
Connection to the company	Be as transparent with company information as you possibly can. Keep your team informed. Share their feedback with peers and your manager, so they feel their voices have been heard.

(continued)

POWER HOUR 19 Handout ❖ **Enlivening Minds at Work**

To Enliven...	Try This...
Energy	Have quick and energetic huddles instead of meetings. Be energetic yourself. Encourage people to get up and move around throughout the day. Hire high-energy people. Help team members manage stress, and make sure no one is working too many hours on a consistent basis.
Participation in team conversations	Ask provocative and evocative questions. Ask for everyone's input, and show gratitude for ideas, even contrary ones. Ask people to comment on topics that you know are of interest to them. Send out questions before meetings, so people can prepare their thoughts.
Collaboration	Ask for team or subteam recommendations. Put people into pairs and small groups to work on projects. Acknowledge and reinforce group accomplishment.

POWER HOUR #19

POWER HOUR 20:
Encouraging Collaboration

Prework Assignment

Find a brief, current article or blog post to share with people as a warm-up to this Power Hour. It's OK, and preferred, if the piece is provocative or controversial. The prework should stir conversation and prime participants for an exploration of the topic.

Learning Objectives

While completing this Power Hour and the application homework, participants will

1. Discuss the importance of team collaboration

2. Identify ways to reinforce collaboration

3. Schedule a collaboration meeting in the coming week.

Trainer's Objective

Trainers will produce a one-hour training session that catalyzes great conversations between managers about management.

Agenda

10 Minutes	Brief discussion of prework (and homework if you are doing these in a series; see chapter 4). Pass out the handout.
15 Minutes	Presentation of the conceptual model or topic
10 Minutes	Initial discussion of the concept using provo/evo questions
15 Minutes	Exercise/application
10 Minutes	Final discussion and assignment of homework

Provo/Evo Discussion Questions

1. What does it mean to collaborate? What does great collaboration look like?

2. Does our work culture encourage collaboration or individual contributions?

3. If someone wants a promotion, are they more likely to get noticed when they collaborate or when they strike out on their own?

4. Are our results suffering because of a lack of collaboration?

Conceptual Model

Most managers will say they want collaboration, but few act consistently with this claim. When you set goals, are they

POWER
HOUR #20

individual or team goals? When you fill out a performance evaluation, are you rating team or individual performance? What's the criteria for promotions, pay raises, and bonuses—individual accomplishment or team accomplishment? I am not suggesting that reinforcing and acknowledging individual excellence is not a good thing—you should reinforce individual excellence. It is important, however, to notice the balance in what you are reinforcing.

People collaborate more when they are given the time; when it is easy to communicate with peers and team members; when they have had the opportunity to work, or practice working, with others; and when they gain a feeling of satisfaction and accomplishment from working together. How many of these conditions exist in your work environment? Managers can help create the place for all these conditions.

Teams who collaborate outperform teams who do not. You will see a significant increase in productivity and results if you increase collaboration. Collaboration is as much a mind-set as it is a set of actions. When team members pool their ideas, thoughts, worries, and talents, they reinforce each other and help protect the team from setbacks. You want this natural process of synergy to flourish in your department because it will serve you and your team well in times of struggle, pressure, or opportunity.

Make sure your actions and words encourage effective collaboration.

Exercise

Split the group into subgroups of three or four. Ask each group to take 10 minutes to brainstorm a list of things managers can do to reinforce collaboration. Ask each group to share its lists.

Homework/Application Assignment

Schedule and hold a team meeting to collaborate on a current or upcoming project or task.

POWER HOUR #20

195

POWER HOUR 20 Handout ❖ Encouraging Collaboration

Most managers will say they want collaboration, but few act consistently with this claim. When you set goals, are they individual or team goals? When you fill out a performance evaluation, are you rating team or individual performance? What's the criteria for promotions, pay raises, and bonuses—individual accomplishment or team accomplishment? I am not suggesting that reinforcing and acknowledging individual excellence is not a good thing—you should reinforce individual excellence. It is important, however, to notice the balance in what you are reinforcing.

People collaborate more when they are given the time, when it is easy to communicate with peers and team members, when they have had the opportunity to work or practice working with others, and when they gain a feeling of satisfaction and accomplishment from working together. How many of these conditions exist in your work environment? Managers can help create the place for all these conditions.

Teams who collaborate outperform teams who do not. You will see a significant increase in productivity and results if you increase collaboration. Collaboration is as much a mind-set as it is a set of actions. When team members pool their ideas, thoughts, worries, and talents, they reinforce each other and help protect the team from setbacks. You want this natural process of synergy to flourish in your department because it will serve you and your team well in times of struggle, pressure, or opportunity.

Make sure your actions and words encourage effective collaboration. Use the following chart to help you.

Ways to Reinforce Collaboration

Contextual Element	Ideas for Reinforcing Collaboration
Physical Location	Seat teams together or in a way that encourages informal conversation. Make sure that you have informal meeting spaces available. If the team is located in more than one place, make sure you get them together on a regular basis and encourage them to use technology to have informal

(continued)

POWER HOUR 20 Handout ❖ Encouraging Collaboration

Contextual Element	Ideas for Reinforcing Collaboration
	and planned conversations. Make sure they have unrestricted access to phone, email, Internet phone, teleconferencing services, and web seminar software.
Communication Processes	Make it a habit to use a portion of your team meetings for collaboration. When people come to your office with questions or ideas, encourage them to get together with a few peers to talk it through (eventually they will do this before coming to you—a beautiful thing).
Tasks and Assignments	Assign projects and tasks to teams, subteams, and peer pairs. Get your team in the habit of working together.
Goals and Measurements	Make sure that at least half of your employees' goals are team, subteam, or pair goals. Use team measures together with individual measures for any evaluations, pay raise considerations, promotions, and bonuses (if you plan to link evaluations to pay raises, which I don't recommend).
Culture	Reinforce and show appreciation for collaborative work. Role-model collaboration by asking team members and peers to work with you on your tasks and projects. Encourage diverse opinions and points of view. Show support when team members get together for informal conversations or meetings.

PART III

Using and Promoting Power Hours

CHAPTER 27

Selling and Launching Power Hour Training

What's Covered in This Chapter

- ❖ Selling the features and benefits of Training Power Hours

- ❖ Marketing Power Hours to managers

- ❖ Aligning your training function to maximize your training impact

Selling the Features and Benefits of Training Power Hours

Let's assume that you are interested in giving Management Training Power Hours a try. Your next question might be,

"How do I enroll key stakeholders?" I use the term *enroll* because it is better to enroll people than it is to merely sell them on an idea. What's the difference? When you sell people on an approach, they agree to do something in the manner you recommend—you have convinced them. That's great, and sometimes that would be our best possible outcome, but selling is not nearly as powerful as enrollment. When you enroll others, they take on the idea or approach as if it were their own. They become emotionally invested in the idea. They become an evangelist for the program or project.

There are a number of things you might do to *sell*:

✓ Offer information that supports your argument or recommendations—persuade with facts.

✓ Share reasoning for recommendation.

✓ Ask for agreement.

And there are a number of things you might do to *enroll* (see sidebar for brief list):

✓ *Acknowledge and get agreement on organizational needs or opportunities, current trends, and barriers.* Create a common understanding for the current situation. Here are some statements you can make that will get people on board in support of Power Hours:

1. We want to continuously build management capabilities to meet the ever-expanding and complex needs of the organization.

2. Managers are busy—a training solution needs to respect the precious nature of time.

3. We want to create an environment where learning occurs in a variety of forums.

4. It is important that management trainers build strong relationships with managers to be most helpful to them as a support function.

5. What are the top two or three organizational development needs based on the goals and strategies of the company?

✓ *Offer information.* Share relevant information that enables others to see all sides of the issue and draw their own conclusions. You can offer relevant information in support of Power Hours:

1. Number and location of managers

2. Results or perceptions of previous training initiatives

3. A primer on informal training

4. Skills and commitment of management trainers.

✓ *Define the opportunity.* What if we could improve development and management effectiveness by using a less schedule-intrusive approach to training? Share what you want to do (give Power Hours a try!) in a way that shows your passion and commitment. If people can see and perceive your energy and drive, it will be contagious. Here are some things you can do:

1. Suggest starting with just a couple small management teams.

2. Offer to transform just one staff meeting per month by using an hour of the meeting for development.

✓ *Share the 4 P's.* Here's the picture, purpose, plan, and their parts. Allow people to become a partner with you in this process. Here are some ways to develop partnerships for informal development conversations like Power Hours:

1. One way to gain enrollment from a key stakeholder is to offer to use his or her management team as a pilot group. Start small and select a Power Hour that you know is going to appeal to this particular functional team.

2. Invite five or six leaders to a brown bag lunch discussion where you demonstrate a Power Hour. Bring in pizza, facilitate the conversation, ask for feedback, and then ask for their support in doing a limited pilot with other managers.

✓ *Invite open and candid dialogue.* You can invite open dialogue about the Power Hours:

1. Ask questions about people's concerns and if there are any reasons why they believe you should not try this approach.

2. Ask for input on the most important management topics or needs that should be addressed in initial Power Hour training sessions.

3. Offer to put them through a Power Hour as a demonstration.

4. Ask for their thoughts about how success should be measured.

✓ *Keep people engaged and informed about the initiative.* You can keep people up-to-date on the Power Hours program in a number of ways:

1. Describe the philosophical foundation for Power Hours: To improve dialogue that makes a difference.

2. Improve the conversations and level of connection you have with key stakeholders.

3. Be open about setbacks and share feedback that you receive from managers—the good, the bad, and the ugly. All feedback is a gift and will allow you to align and tweak your Power Hour plan and offerings.

Ways to Enroll Support for Your Initiative

❖ Acknowledge and get agreement on organizational needs or opportunities, current trends, and barriers.

❖ Offer information.

❖ Define the opportunity.

❖ Share the 4 P's.

❖ Invite open and candid dialogue.

❖ Keep people engaged and informed about the initiative.

Getting enrollment for trying Management Training Power Hours should not be too difficult because the approach is easy to try and it meets managers' needs. Another approach to gaining enrollment might be to put key stakeholders through a Power Hour before explaining what they are and how you want to use them to train managers. Seeing, feeling, and experiencing Power Hours is powerful and will improve enrollment.

Marketing Power Hours to Managers

Managers will love the way Power Hours fit into their schedule, and they will love the interactive and relevant nature of each of the topics discussed. Before you begin facilitating Power Hours, though, have a 20-minute meeting with managers to tell them about the plan and ask for their input and suggestions:

❖ The times and days that will be best for their Power Hour sessions.

❖ The topics that they feel would be most helpful. (You should have a list with examples and ask for other topics not listed.)

❖ The most convenient location for each of the meetings.

❖ How often the Power Hours should be offered and whether topics ought to be repeated.

Keep this meeting short. You want to demonstrate that you believe their time is precious and that you do not intend to waste it. This type of conversation will go a long way toward helping you enroll your clients—managers—in the Power Hour approach to training.

Aligning Your Training Function to Maximize Your Training Impact

Your key stakeholders are enrolled. Managers can't wait to get started. Great! Now you need to make sure that you have set up your training function for success. Here are several ways you can align your training department to provide excellent Power Hour training:

❖ *Practice the first couple of Power Hour units within the training department.* Let everyone experience the product and offer input on how to tweak the design for your company.

❖ *Don't over schedule your trainers.* If your management trainers are booked up with full-day training assignments, they will not be able to seize training opportunities to offer Power Hours as the opportunities present themselves. Power Hour training is a nimble and flexible model, so your trainers need to have some flexibility in their schedules.

❖ *Be service oriented to a fault.* Offer to provide the Power Hours when and how managers request them—go where the energy is, even if it means coming in on weekends or in the evenings. Offer to bring in a pizza for a lunchtime brown bag session. Once your managers are sold on the model, they will be more inclined to work with you on a win-win training schedule.

Using Management Training Power Hours requires you and your team to be flexible, approachable, and responsive. These are qualities that all great service teams have anyway, so it is likely that this approach will fit well into your current department practices.

What to Do Next

❖ Facilitate a couple of Power Hours within your training and HR department—be your own guinea pigs!

❖ Start putting together the information you need to enroll key stakeholders and managers. Enlist evangelists.

CHAPTER 28

A Year-Long Management Training Curriculum

What's Covered in This Chapter

- ❖ Reasons to create a plan for the whole year
- ❖ Sample course offerings
- ❖ Sample schedules

Why Create a Plan for the Whole Year?

What if you gave the Power Hour concept of management a try for a year? What would your plan look like, and what should you expect in terms of impact? First, I think your training would become very focused and dynamic. Most important, you would raise the level of conversation occurring in your company. When conversations are great, decisions and actions improve.

I would like to encourage you to create a year-long management training plan using Power Hours. It is helpful to plan ahead because offering Power Hours requires different training processes and resources than does a schedule of traditional classes. Doing these informal sessions with small groups can be a logistical challenge in larger companies. Further, your management trainers need to be ready, willing, and able to be conversation catalysts and spend much more of their time facilitating small group conversations (this is time well spent!). You should also plan trainer time to seek provocative and evocative prework and create Power Hours for topics I have not addressed in this book.

Sample Course Offerings

This book offers 20 Power Hours that address fundamental management topics. To create a year of high-impact training, add Power Hours that address needs specific to your business or managers. Do you work for a company that regularly develops and introduces new products? If so, add a few Power Hours to discuss what's state-of-the-art in product development, innovation, and project management. Is your company a service provider facing new or strong competition? Then, create Power Hours that address the various elements of service excellence. Is your company suffering from high turnover? If so, you can create Power Hours that help managers improve employee retention. And when it is time to head into next year's budgeting process, add one or two Power Hours that address specific elements of the magic and art of budgeting.

To create a Power Hour, I isolate one concept or tool that I think is helpful and build a conversation around the tool. It is important to resist the urge to present more than one topic during a Power Hour. Don't offer a list of 10 skills and then expect the conversation to make a difference. Power Hours go narrow and deep on a topic versus wide and shallow. Here are a few examples of good and bad Power Hour topics:

✓ *Good:* What does job fit mean?

✓ *Bad:* Employee relations skills

✓ *Good:* Seeing constraints

✓ *Bad:* Process Improvement

✓ *Good:* Winning habits for improving budget accuracy

✓ *Bad:* Review of this year's budgeting process and deadlines

Great conversations go deep, and the more managers talk about the business in meaningful terms, the more useful the conversations will be in helping them produce results. I get very impatient when I see facilitators of staff meeting after staff meeting breeze through a long list of topics. Each topic receives so little conversation that the time is wasted. Power Hours can be the bright spot in management conversations and lead to deeper dialogue in other meetings.

Sample Schedules

You are ready to define a year-long plan for training managers using Power Hours—great! To help get your creative juices flowing, I offer two sample schedules for you to consider and modify. The biggest factors are the size and location(s) of your management population and the number of trainers you have to conduct the Power Hours.

Using Power Hours: One per Month

The first schedule, shown in Example 28.1, offers a slow training pace. This is most appropriate if you have a large group of managers and therefore need to do each Power Hour many times or in different locations. Notice that I suggest some of the more

Example 28.1 ❖ Using Power Hours: One per Month

Month	POWER HOUR	Month	POWER HOUR
January	4: Your Management A-B Boxes	July	12: Meetings That Rock!
February	5: Your Management Filter	August	13: Mastering Your Time
March	7: Grand Slam Home Run	September	16: Knowing When and How to Say "No"
April	8: Defining Excellence	October	10: The Art of Planning
May	9: Communicating Expectations	November	17: Aligning Your Department for Success
June	11: Results-Oriented Responses	December	15: Your Leadership Legacy

reflective Power Hours for the beginning and end of the year, when it's a good time to self-evaluate alignment and progress to goals.

Using Power Hours: Two per Month

The second schedule, shown in Example 28.2, is perfect for smaller or more nimble organizations that are ready to zoom forward, have fewer managers to train, and have at least one management trainer dedicated to support the plan. Using Power Hours twice a month keeps the management conversation alive and kicking! My preference would be to provide a new Power Hour every two weeks.

Example 28.2 ❖ Using Powers Hours: Two per Month

Month	POWER HOUR	Month	POWER HOUR
January	1: Management in the Modern Times *AND* 2: What's Expected of You	July	12: Meetings That Rock! *AND* A Power Hour You Create
February	4: Your Management A-B Boxes *AND* 5: Your Management Filter	August	13: Mastering Your Time *AND* 16: Knowing When and How to Say "No"
March	7: Grand Slam Home Runs *AND* 8: Defining Excellence	September	14: Internal Service Excellence *AND* A Power Hour You Create
April	6: Mind Your Metrics! *AND* 9: Communicating Expectations	October	10: The Art of Planning *AND* 17: Aligning Your Department for Success
May	19: Enlivening Minds at Work *AND* 20: Encouraging Collaboration	November	18: The Art of Employee One-on-Ones *AND* A Power Hour You Create
June	11: Results-Oriented Responses *AND* A Power Hour You Create	December	15: Your Leadership Legacy *AND* 3: Managing and Improving Your Reputation

What to Do Next

❖ Come up with a unique plan that suits your company's needs. If the business conversations are excellent and the topics are highly relevant, you almost can't go wrong. Let Management Training Power Hours enliven and align your management training function for success.

CHAPTER 29

Conclusion

As management trainers, we want to see the dial move on management success, and we want to know that our efforts have contributed to positive results. Management is a craft—a set of skills, competencies, and practices that are cultivated over time. Management training should support managers as they build their craft and grow as managers and leaders.

One-time events or infrequent multiday training sessions are great for getting development conversations started, but they come with a big downside for managers. Once the training class is over, managers hear the call of their mile-long do-to lists, and lessons learned in training are often set aside. Their good intentions give way to operational needs that have built up while they were attending the training class. Many managers want training, but they find that taking a day or week away from their departments too difficult. We don't want managers to feel punished for attending our training, do we?

Power Hours take less time and at the same time keep the focus on development. For a craft to be built, development conversations must continue throughout the year. Training Power Hours offer management-training professionals a way to ensure a lively and productive dialogue about great management practices and tools. You have heard the saying "Out of sight, out of mind," right? The same is true for training and development. If development conversations are infrequent, they will be forgotten.

As training professionals, we are asked to do more with less—just like all the other departments. Training Power Hours require a more intimate approach than many other programs— but are otherwise a very low-cost training solution. You do not need to pay high licensing fees, create expensive training materials, or build fancy training facilities. Power Hours are high touch, low tech, and adaptable. Training offerings can be tailored to best meet current managerial challenges and opportunities.

Training Power Hours can be used as the foundation for a management-training program (my preference) or to complement other more traditional training programs. Because they require a personal, high-touch approach, they enable management trainers to build stronger relationships with managers. This relationship will help the training department understand development needs and align training plans to achieve better results.

Management is a social act. Management training is also a social act. It occurs in conversation and through relationships. Management Training Power Hours will help you maximize your management training efforts and impact the organization's success.

I hope you give Management Training Power Hours a try! I would love to hear your stories and answer any questions you have about using Power Hours. You can contact me through my website at www.lisahaneberg.com.

Using the Compact Disc

The compact disc includes all the Power Hour handouts and worksheets for the book. Feel free to modify any of the materials to suit your needs. I recommend that you keep each Power Hour handout to one page (or two pages copied back to back on one piece of paper). Here are the Power Hour handouts and other materials you'll find on the CD:

Socratic Questions (Chapter 3)

Management Training Dashboard (Chapter 5)

Starter List of Blogs (Chapter 6)

Power Hour 1 Handout: Management in the Modern Times

Power Hour 2 Handout: What's Expected of You

Power Hour 3 Handout: Managing and Improving Your Reputation

Power Hour 4 Handout: Your Management A-B Boxes

ABOUT THE AUTHOR

Lisa Haneberg is an expert in the areas of management, leadership, and personal and organizational success. She consults in the areas of organization development, management and leadership training, and human resources. Haneberg also offers integrated training solutions and individual and group coaching services. She is an enthusiastic, fun presenter and speaker, available to address a variety of leadership and management topics.

Her first book, *High Impact Middle Management: Solutions for Today's Busy Managers* was a groundbreaking management book for professional middle managers (Adams Media, 2005). She has also written *Focus Like a Laser Beam: Ten Ways to Do What Matters Most* (Jossey Bass, 2006), *Two Weeks to a Breakthrough: How to Zoom Toward Your Goals in 14 Days or Less* (Jossey Bass, 2007), *Organization Development Basics* (ASTD, 2005), *Coaching Basics* (ASTD, 2006), and *10 Steps to Be a*

Successful Manager (ASTD, 2007). Lisa reaches a worldwide audience through her popular management blog called *Management Craft* (www.managementcraft.com). Management Craft offers resources and perspectives to leaders, managers, and those who develop and coach them. Her main website, www.lisahaneberg.com, highlights her products and services.

Over the past 25 years, Lisa has worked with leaders at all levels and for organizations of many types and sizes, including high-tech manufacturing (Intel); distribution, manufacturing, and services (Black & Decker, Mead Paper, Corbis); e-retailing and distribution (Amazon.com); travel and leisure products and services (Beacon Hotel, Travcoa, and Cruise West); and the Royal Government of Thailand. She earned an undergraduate degree in Behavioral Sciences from the University of Maryland and has taken graduate courses at Johns Hopkins University, Ohio State University, and Goddard College.

Lisa Haneberg lives in the beautiful Pacific Northwest with her husband, cat, and four dogs. She enjoys travel, reading, writing, and driving her motorcycle down winding roads.

INDEX

Note: A *t* following a page reference indicates a table; *f* indicates a figure.